COMPENSATION
THE VICTIM'S PERSPECTIVE

Compensation. The Victim's Perspective
J.D.W.E. Mulder

ISBN: 978-90-5850-956-7

Published by:
Wolf Legal Publishers (WLP)
PO Box 313
5060 AH Oisterwijk
The Netherlands
E-Mail: info@wolfpublishers.nl
www.wolfpublishers.com

COMPENSATION
THE VICTIM'S PERSPECTIVE

Proefschrift ter verkrijging van de graad van doctor aan Tilburg University op gezag van de rector magnificus, prof. dr. Ph. Eijlander, in het openbaar te verdedigen ten overstaan van een door het college voor promoties aangewezen commissie in de aula van de Universiteit op vrijdag 8 maart 2013 om 14.15 uur door Johanna Dirkina Wilhelmina Elisabeth Mulder geboren op 18 november 1978 te Alkmaar.

Promotores:

Prof. mr. M.S. Groenhuijsen
Prof. dr. E.E.C. van Damme

Promotiecommissie:

Prof. dr. mr. J.J.M. van Dijk
Prof. dr. M.G. Faure
Prof. dr. J.A.P. Hagenaars
Prof. mr. S.D. Lindenbergh
Dr. B.A. Vollaard

Opgedragen aan N.C. Mulder

Persoonlijke noot van de auteur

De afgelopen jaren waren mooie jaren, zeer mooie jaren zelfs. Ik kon mijn ziel en zaligheid kwijt in dit proefschrift, het werken aan de Universiteit van Tilburg bracht me nieuwe vrienden, bij Intervict ontmoette ik mijn grote liefde en als klap op de vuurpijl mocht ik vorig jaar een geweldig lief meisje op de wereld zetten. Ik kijk dan ook met veel plezier terug op mijn 'proefschrifttijd'. En niet in de laatste plaats ben ik trots op het werk dat hier nu ligt.

Al de stukken die ik geschreven heb gaan over het vergoeden van schade. Het was begin 2007 dat ik min of meer toevallig op dit onderwerp stuitte. Ik had zitten surfen op het internet en was via via op de website van het Schadefonds Geweldsmisdrijven beland. Daar las ik dat het Schadefonds jaarlijks miljoenen euro's uitkeert aan slachtoffers van ernstige misdrijven als poging tot moord, verkrachting en zware mishandeling. Onmiddellijk borrelden er allerlei vragen bij me op. Wat betekent geld voor mensen die zo zwaar geleden hebben? Verwachten ze veel geld te krijgen of zijn ze tevreden met een klein bedrag? En wat is de reden dat het Schadefonds, dat onderdeel is van de Nederlandse overheid, een financiële vergoeding aan deze slachtoffers geeft? Toen ik op zoek ging naar een antwoord op deze vragen kwam ik erachter dat er nauwelijks iets bekend was over het vergoeden van schade. De keuze was toen snel gemaakt: ik zou hier zelf onderzoek naar gaan doen!

Uiteindelijk heb ik vijf jaar met veel plezier aan het onderwerp van schadevergoeding gewerkt. Zelfs nu het werk erop zit, boeit het onderwerp me nog steeds. Het is zo tastbaar, iedereen begrijpt waar het over gaat. Tegelijkertijd roept het zoveel 'grote' vragen op; waarom plegen mensen bijvoorbeeld (ernstige) misdrijven? Wat zijn de gevolgen van die misdrijven voor slachtoffers? Welk doel hebben slachtoffers voor ogen als zij naar de rechter stappen? En waarom hebben we eigenlijk een rechtssysteem?

Als econoom was het erg interessant om met al deze vragen bezig te zijn. Het heeft me in contact gebracht met tal van verschillende mensen en ik heb kennis uit uiteenlopende wetenschappelijke hoeken kunnen opdoen. Ik ben het International Victimology Institute Tilburg (Intervict) en in het bijzonder Marc Groenhuijsen en Rianne Letschert, dan ook zeer dankbaar dat ze me de mogelijkheid hebben geboden dit proefschrift te schrijven en bovenal de vrijheid hebben gegund dat op mijn eigen manier te doen.

Ook Eric van Damme ben ik ontzettend dankbaar. Het is inmiddels meer dan zes jaar geleden dat ik hem aansprak op een congres met de vraag of hij eens met me van gedachten zou willen wisselen over een mogelijk promotieonderwerp. Tot mijn blijdschap was hij daartoe bereid en zo raakte het balletje aan het rollen. Uiteindelijk is hij één van mijn begeleiders geworden en heeft hij mijn werk steeds nauwlettend in de gaten gehouden. Aan de hand van zijn opmerkingen heb ik mijn gedachten kunnen ontwikkelen en mijn werk kunnen verbeteren. Bovendien heeft hij me in goede en slechte tijden met raad en daad bijgestaan. Ik had me dan ook werkelijk geen betere begeleider kunnen wensen.

Het Schadefonds Geweldsmisdrijven mag ook niet onvermeld blijven. Immers, zonder hun medewerking had mijn onderzoek in het geheel niet uitgevoerd kunnen worden. Ik ben blij verrast geweest door hun open houding en de bereidheid me verder te helpen. Hetzelfde geldt voor de slachtoffers die zo vriendelijk zijn geweest mijn vragenlijst in te vullen. Mijn dank is groot.

Verder zijn er al die lieve mensen die de afgelopen jaren al mijn geklets over schadevergoeding en slachtoffers hebben moeten aanhoren en nooit één kik gegeven hebben. Sterker nog, velen van jullie wisten de indruk te wekken dat ik niet de enige was die het allemaal erg interessant vond. Zonder jullie, mijn lieve vrienden, had ik dan ook nooit met zo veel plezier aan dit boek kunnen werken en dus ben ik ook jullie zeer dankbaar. Ik hoop dat ik nog heel veel jaren mag genieten van jullie aangename gezelschap!

Speciale woorden van dank zijn er voor mijn lieve tante Marjon. Ze heeft me in de loop der jaren het gevoel weten te geven dat er plek is waar ik altijd welkom ben en er onvoorwaardelijk van me gehouden wordt. Samen met ome Cees en mijn lieve neefjes heeft zij me dan ook iets gegeven waar ik de rest van mijn leven mee vooruit kan. En wat kan een mens zich nog meer wensen, dan dit soort familie te hebben?

Aan een ander familielid wil ik dit proefschrift opdragen; Nic Mulder, mijn vader. Zijn dood is het ergste dat me ooit is overkomen en de gevolgen ervan zijn tot op de dag van vandaag merkbaar. Toch is blijdschap het gevoel dat overheerst als ik aan hem denk. Hij was een geweldige vader en ik ben trots op het feit dat ik zijn dochter ben. Ik had graag gezien dat hij dit boek had kunnen inkijken en bij de verdediging op de eerste rij had gezeten. Jammer genoeg is ons dat niet gegeven. In mijn hart is hij echter altijd bij me en ik draag mijn proefschrift dan ook met liefde aan hem op.

De afsluitende woorden van deze persoonlijke noot zijn voor de twee mensen die ik het meest lief heb; Antony en Eve Pemberton, mijn geweldige man en mijn lieve dochter. Waar ik ook ben met jullie, thuis op de bank, in het bos, op het terras of 's ochtends in bed, we zijn blij en hebben plezier. Dat het zo simpel kan zijn om geluk te ervaren had ik nooit kunnen bedenken. Jullie zijn de mensen met wie ik het liefste samen ben en ik hoop dan ook dat ik nog vele mooie jaren mag blijven.

Augustus 2012,

José Mulder

Table of contents

General introduction 1
1. Background 1
2. Outline 3
3. Suggestions for further research 6
References 7

How to compensate a victim's losses? An economic perspective 11
Abstract 11
Introduction 11
1. Making whole 13
1.1. A victim's well-being 14
1.2. How losses affect one's well-being 15
2.1. Insurance of economic losses 19
2.2. Insurance of non-economic losses 20
2.3. Discussion on demand for pain and suffering insurance 21
3. Other means to compensation 23
3.1. Why plaintiffs go to court 23
3.2. Procedural utility 24
3.3. How does this relate to insurance theory? 24
3.4. Taking non-economic factors into account 25
4. Questions that remain 26
Summary 27
References 28

Financial compensation for victims of crime 35
Introduction 35
1. Methodology 37
1.1. The Dutch Crime Compensation Fund 37
1.2. The respondents 39
1.3. The survey 40
2. Results 42
2.1. Characteristics of recipients and their victimization 42
2.1.1. Type of crime 42
2.1.3. Recipient's Gender 45
2.1.4. Recipients' nationality 46
2.1.5. Recipients' income 47
2.1.6. Do recipients know the offender? 47
2.1.7. Summary 48
2.2. The procedure 48
2.3. Before applying 49
2.3.1. How did victims learn about the possibility to apply? 49
2.3.2. Time passed since the offence 49
2.3.3. The application itself 51
2.3.4. Looking back on the decision 54
2.3.5. Summary 56
2.4. Financial awards 56
2.5. Total award 57
2.5.1. Economic compensation 58
2.5.2. Compensation for pain and suffering 59
2.6. Summary 61
2.7. Therapeutic effects and social value 62

2.7.1. Acknowledgement and justice 62
2.7.2. Emotional support and coping 63
2.7.3. Confirmation of innocence 65
2.8. Social value of money? 65
2.9. Summary 66
3. Summary & conclusion 67
References 69
Appendix I: Questionnaire 73

Victims' satisfaction with compensation: how procedure matters 81
Introduction 81
1. Methodology 83
1.1. The Dutch Crime Compensation Fund 83
1.2. The study 84
1.3. Sample 85
1.3.1. Non-response 86
2. Results 87
2.1. Compensation 87
2.2. Expectations 88
2.3. Are recipients satisfied with the Fund's awards? 89
2.3.1. Why are victims satisfied? 90
2.4. What does satisfaction actually entail? 92
2.4.1. Again: Why are recipients satisfied? 95
2.4.2. Procedural satisfaction 97
3. Discussion and conclusion 99
References 101
Appendix A: statistical analysis 105
References 109

The symbolic value of financial compensation 111
Introduction 111
1.1. Dutch Crime Compensation Fund 113
1.2. The study 114
1.3. The sample 115
1.3.1. Non-response 117
2. Results 117
2.1. Victims' reasons to apply for compensation 117
2.2. Knowledge about state's involvement 118
2.3. Symbolic affect 118
2.3.1. Interrelatedness of symbolic variables 120
2.3.2. What affects the symbolic value of compensation? 122
3. Discussion & conclusion 124
References 125
Appendix 1 128
Appendix 2 130

A new economic perspective on victims of crime: homo reciprocans 133
Introduction 133
1. A victim of crime as homo economicus 135
2. A psycholocigal perspective on victims of crime 137
3. homo reciprocans 139
4. Conclusion: Victims of crime as homo reciprocans 141
References 143

"On the most basic level, what we are trying to do in science is to understand our world. Predictions are an excellent means of testing our comprehension, and once we have the comprehension, applications are inevitable; but the basic aim of scientific activity remains the comprehension itself"

Robert Aumann (1985, p. 29)

General introduction

Compensation, the victims' perspective is my PhD-thesis. It is a body of work with which I hope to prove worthy of carrying that title. It contains five chapters, which all concern the topic of victim compensation.

1. Background

In the spring of 2007, I came across the website of the Dutch Crime Compensation Fund (het Schadefonds Geweldsmisdrijven).[1] I had never heard of this state-run fund before, but was immediately intrigued by its objective: offering financial support to victims of violent crime. It made me wonder what receiving money means to people who have been severely victimized. Would a victim of attempted murder agree with Ecclesiastes (10:19),for example, that "money is the answer for everything"?[2] Or would one perceive financial support as merely symbolic?

In order to find more information on victim compensation I continued surfing the web. Soon I discovered that state-run crime compensation funds exist all over the globe (see O'Connell, 2003 for an overview). Surprisingly little information was available on how state compensation affects its recipients, though. Moreover, I could hardly find empirical research on the effects of financial compensation in general. Due to this dearth of research on victim compensation, I decided to conduct a study in this field myself.

Having a background in economics, I started my research by studying the economic literature on compensation. It turned out there was surprisingly little; most economists view the legal system as a means to deter future accidents and crimes (e.g. Becker, 1968; Polinksy & Shavell, 1998; Cooter & Rubinfield, 1989). As a consequence, relatively few scholars have taken victims, or victim compensation, into account.[3] The paraphrase of Faure's rather bold claim is illustrative: 'legal economists protect victims by making sure there are less of them' (1999, p. D20).

The economists that have studied victim compensation generally perceive it to be a matter of insurance. Following Calabresi (1970) they accept the

---

1 The website of the Dutch Crime Compensation Fund is: http://www.schadefonds.nl/en_GB/.

2 The complete phrase is: "A feast is made for laughter, and wine makes life merry, but money is the answer for everything". New International Translation of the Bible, 1984.

3 Victims have not been taken account by economists and other economically oriented scholars due to the fact that one studies crime from an ex ante perspective. This traditional economic view holds that one studies how potential offenders can be deterred from committing crime. In other words, scholars study how there will be less victims (see paraphrase of Faure, 1999) and not how one should deal with the persons who actually do fall victim to crime.

paradigm whereby the court system and first-party insurance markets act like alternative solutions to the problem of allocating victims' losses (see Frech, 1994; Cooter, 1991; Viscusi, 1996). One, therefore, states that the optimal level of compensation awarded in court should equal the efficient level of actuarially fair insurance -which is the coverage an independent, rational and fully informed consumer would have bought in a world without tort law- (see Viscusi, 2000a, p. 121; Shavell, 2003, ch. 5, p. 10).

This thought experiment leads to the conclusion that economic losses (losses that have substitutes or that can be repaired) should be compensated fully, while non-economic losses (pain and suffering) should not be compensated at all (see Cook & Graham, 1977; Friedman, 1982, Arlen 2000; Shavell, 2003; Kaplow & Shavell, 2002; Viscusi 1996). Within the legal literature, these conclusions have been heavily debated (see Croley & Hanson, 1995; Avraham, 2003; Feldman, 1996), but the 'insurance theory' has remained the leading theory for those studying compensation, nevertheless (see Viscusi, 2000, p. 116; Visscher, 2009, p. 11; VandenBerghe, 2010, p. 61).[4]

Scholars from other disciplines, like legal psychology and victimology, purport quite a different view on the reparation of victims' losses. Instead of addressing it as a mere financial matter they stress the symbolic value of compensation and the importance of the procedures by which compensation levels are set (see Tyler & Thorisdottir, 2003). Cobley (1998, p. 222), for example, argues that compensation serves as a public statement of recognition; not only that the crime took place, but also that someone other than the victim was responsible. Non-financial matters like these are said to be of great importance to victims (see Tyler & Thorisdottir, 2003).

The conflicting scholarly views on compensation brought me back to my initial question namely: how do victims themselves perceive financial reparation? Is money their only concern when they file for compensation? Are they perhaps expecting to be awarded millions of euro's? Or do victims care at least as much about non-financial matters, like acknowledgement and recognition?

As noted above, very few empirical studies have been done so far in the field of financial reparation. So in order to learn more about victims' attitudes towards financial compensation, I conducted a survey among recipients of the Dutch Crime Compensation Fund myself. According to its results, a large majority of recipients is satisfied with the rather modest amounts of reparation granted by the Dutch Crime Compensation Fund (on average 2070 euro for pain and suffering and 1050 euro for economic losses) (see chapter 2 and 3). Moreover, a majority of respondents contributes symbolic value to the money received (see chapter 4).

4 Not all economists dealing with compensation issues have taken the insurance perspective, yet they do come to similar conclusions (see for example Friedman, 1982 and 2000).

These results are difficult to interpret by means of the economic theory of insurance. After all, contrary to the assumptions underlying this theory, the survey results indicate that receiving financial reparation entails more to victims than just a simple financial deed (see chapter 3 and 4). The insurance analogy, therefore, seems to misrepresent the case at hand. Contemporary work of behavioral and experimental economists, however, offers an promising alternative framework for the study of victims and victims' compensation: 'homo reciprocans'.

As I will describe in chapter 5, 'homo reciprocans' is the result of numerous studies that have shown how humans tend to reward positive acts of others and to punish negative ones, even when punishment is at a cost (see for an overview Fehr & Fishbacher, 2003). This reciprocal behavior is notably in line with that of victims of crime; according to extensive psychological research victims have a strong need to retaliate. Or as Miller (1993, p. 16), puts it: incurring losses due to the harmful acts of others is like 'receiving gifts of negative moral value, which demand *repayment*'. Based on these economic and psychological findings, I argue in chapter 5 that the work of contemporary economists provides a promising framework for the ongoing study of victim issues.

All in all, the topic of victim compensation is being considered from various angles throughout this thesis. Some chapters are primarily theoretical, others mainly empirical. Yet, all are explorative of nature. As a result this thesis is the representation of my curiosity and fascination for the topic of victim compensation. And hopefully, by offering the victim's perspective, it will contribute to a better understanding of how financial reparation affects those who suffer due to the intentional acts of others.

2. Outline

As explained, *Compensation, the victims' perspective*, contains five chapters. Below I will describe the contents of each chapter briefly. But before I do so, I would like to stress that the chapters are primarily to be read as stand-alone documents. Each chapter has been, or will be, submitted to a scientific journal for peer review and publication. Consequently, and inevitably, the chapters are subject to repetitions.

Chapter 1: How to compensate a victim's losses? An economic perspective.

The first chapter expounds the framework that is used by economic scholars to analyze the effects of financial compensation. The starting point for economic analysis is a victim's well-being, expressed in terms of utility. Since an individual's well-being is negatively affected by the sustainment of a loss, victims experience less utility from life and wealth than they did before a crime or accident. Making victims whole by awarding them financial compensation, therefore, implies that victims should be offered an amount of money that offsets one's utility loss. According to renowned economists, there is just one method to determine the appropriate amount of compensatory damages, and that is by assessing the amount of first-party insurance that a victim would have bought voluntarily (on an actuarially fair basis) in a world without tort law (Viscusi, 1996, p. 153; Shavell, 2003, ch. 5, p. 10). In this chapter, however, it will be argued that insurance theory falls short in determining damages due to its focus on financial compensation. Many empirical studies have shown how "litigants are propelled into litigation as a result not only of material but also psychological and emotional needs to alleviate the effects of distressing experiences" (Relis, 2006, p. 193; see Huver et al., 2007 for similar conclusions). By just focussing on financial matters, like the insurance theory does, one disregards these other, sometimes even more important needs. That while financial and non-financial forms of compensation are closely related, and both fit the economic framework of well-being.

Chapter 2: *Financial compensation for victims of crime. Who receives compensation from the Dutch Crime Compensation Fund and how do these victims perceive financial compensation?*

The second chapter of this thesis describes the general results of the survey I conducted among recipients of the Dutch Crime Compensation Fund. Since the effects of granting public funds to victims of violent crime have hardly been studied up till now (O'Connell, 2003, p. 20-1), this chapter offers valuable insight in the matter of state compensation. Among others, it provides information on the persons who are granted state compensation, the procedure these persons have gone through, whether recipients are satisfied with the amounts of money awarded and finally, the symbolic value of state compensation.

Chapter 3: *Victims' satisfaction with compensation: how procedure matters*

Chapter 3 offers an in-depth analysis of results discussed in chapter 2. It explores recipients' satisfaction with the money granted to them by the Dutch Crime Compensation Fund. By means of several statistical analyses, the chapter expounds how recipients' satisfaction with the compensation received coincides with other outcome related variables. Moreover, it shows how satisfaction can be distinguished in outcome and procedural related factors. Surprisingly enough, neither of these factors correlates with financial variables like the amount of money received or one's income. Procedural variables, on the other hand, like the time it takes the Fund to decide on one's case and how many times victims have been in contact with the Fund, do affect recipients' satisfaction. All and all, chapter 3 shows how the exact amount of compensation awarded by the Crime Compensation Fund is not as important to victims as often assumed; victims are far more concerned with the procedural aspects of being compensated.

Chapter 4: *The symbolic value of money. An empirical analysis of victim compensation.*

Chapter 4 offers an in-depth analysis of the results presented in chapter 2 regarding the symbolic value of compensation. It has often been asserted that state compensation represents symbolic value; it would for instance 'serve symbolically to reforge the bonds that bind people together' (Dignan, 2005, p. 44). Subsequently, state compensation is said to give victims a sense of empowerment, validation and integration into the social order (Young, 2003). Freckelton (2004) even speaks about a "therapeutically symbolic gesture of collegiality and concern" (p. 58-9). Yet, despite the fact that state compensation schemes have been granting public money to victims of crime for several decades now, it has remained unknown whether state compensation truly represents symbolic value to those receiving it. Chapter 4, therefore, provides the first empirical evidence that suggests that state compensation has indeed symbolic value. Several different symbolic values have been studied, and according to the data-analysis they reflect two general values, namely internal and external symbolic value. Further analysis shows that financial matters do not affect symbolic value. Knowledge about the state's involvement, however, does. Victims, who are aware of the state's involvement, score significantly higher on both symbolic factors than do victims who do not know they received public money.

Chapter 5: *A new perspective on victims of crime: homo reciprocans*

Chapter 5 examines how research on victim compensation might benefit from contemporary economic research. As explained in chapter 1, economic scholars have used the analogy of insurance to determine appropriate levels of victim compensation. This analogy is based on the assumption that humans, and thus victims, behave as if they are 'homo economicus': rational and narrowly self-interested actors. According to extensive psychological research, on the other hand, victims of crime are not in the least concerned with their own material self-interest; they primarily care about their social standing and how they might reestablish the social balance. As a result, retaliation and punishment are foremost in their minds. Interestingly enough, contemporary economic studies lead to similar conclusions. There is a broad range of behavioral and experimental work that shows how people tend to reward positive acts of others and to punish negative ones, even when it is at a cost. Due to this reciprocal type of behavior, one even speaks of 'homo reciprocans' instead of 'homo economicus' (see Fehr & Gachter, 1998; Dohmen, Falk, Huffman & Sunde, 2009).

By showing how victims' behavior is notably in line with that of 'homo reciprocans', I hope to persuade economically oriented scholars to replace their perspective of 'homo economicus' for that of 'homo reciprocans'. Moreover, I hope to show with this chapter that experimental and behavioral economics provides an promising framework for further research on victim compensation.

3. Suggestions for further research

Compensation issues have received little attention up till now. As a result, many research questions remain. Throughout the chapters of this thesis several of them are mentioned, but here too, I would like to do some suggestions for further research.

First of all, a theoretical framework for state compensation, is still lacking. Many countries, all over the globe, have state-run compensation funds, some for even more than three decades, yet it is unclear what one is trying to accomplish with these funds. Subsequently, it is not possible to determine whether state compensation funds work effectively and efficiently. Nor are there any guidelines to assess how recipients (and those who are denied compensation) are affected by the state's involvement, and whether their expectations are in line with a Funds' goals.

Secondly, it might be interesting to see how compensation schemes differ from each other, and if and how that affects recipients. The British Criminal Injuries Compensation Authority, for example, is known for its generous awards (ranging between £1.000 and £500.000), while the Criminal Injuries Compensation Board in Ontario, Canada, organizes (public) hearings in order to assess victims' applications. Do these and other differences matter for recipients? Or will they evaluate all funds similarly?

Thirdly, the survey among recipients of the Dutch Crime Compensation Fund shows how victims wait on average 20 months before they apply for compensation. Unfortunately, it was not possible to provide an explanation for this rather long period. Hence, the question remains whether it is due to a lack of knowledge that victims do not apply shortly after the incident, or that perhaps they prefer justice to take its course first.

According to the survey results the exact amount of money awarded to victims of violent crime is not that important. People who are granted relatively high amounts, for example, are not more satisfied than others, nor do they contribute more symbolic value to the Fund's money. In other words, recipients of state compensation seem to be happy with relatively little. Yet, it seems likely that too little compensation could be taken as an offence. Hence, it might be interesting to see whether there exists something like an optimal level of compensation.

Furthermore, the symbolic value of money, deserves more attention too, I believe. My research shows that recipients of state compensation attribute symbolic value to the money they receive: it helps them to cope with the emotional consequences of the crime for example. Yet, it might be worthwhile to examine this in more detail. For example, why do recipients attribute symbolic value? Would any financial award convey the message that someone actually believes them? Or are there other important factors which result in the attribution of symbolic value?

Finally, I would like to mention the victims whose application for compensation was denied. How does such a rejection affect them? Is being denied compensation, for example, a signal of disbelief, or do only the financial consequences matter? And why are victims denied compensation in the first place? Is it simply because they do not bother to provide all the requested information[5] (according to the Dutch Crime Compensation Fund most denied applications are the result of missing information), or are there other explanations? And how does a rejection of one's application influence one's appreciation of the Fund, or for that matter, the state?

References

Arlen, J., (2000), Tort Damages, in B. Bouckaert en G. De Geest, eds., Encyclopaedia of Law and Economics, Vol. II, pp. 682-734, Edward Elgar; Cheltenham.

Aumann, R. (1985), What Is Game Theory Trying to Accomplish? In *Frontiers of Economics*, K. Arrow and S. Honkapohja (eds). Oxford: Basil Blackwell, p. 29.

Avraham, R. (2003). *Pain-and-suffering damages in tort law: revisiting the theoretical framework and the empirical data*. Michigan Law and Economics Research Paper No. 03-001; Northwestern Law & Econ Research Paper No. 03-03.

Becker, G.S. (1968), Crime and punishment: an economic approach. *The Journal of Political Economy*, 76(2), pp. 169-217.

5 According to the Dutch Crime Compensation Fund the majority of denied applications are caused by applicants who provide incomplete information.

Calabresi, G. (1970), The Cost of Accidents: A Legal and Economic Analysis. New Haven, CT: Yale University Press.

Cobley, C. (1998). Financial compensation for victims of child abuse. *Journal of Social Welfare and Family Law*, 20(3), pp. 221-235.

Cook, P. J. & Graham, D.A. (1977). The demand for insurance and protection: the case of irreplaceable commodities. *The Quarterly Journal of Economics*, 91(1), pp. 143-156.
Cooter, R.D. & Rubinfeld, D.L. (1989): Economic analysis of legal disputes and their resolution. *Journal of Economic Literature*, 27, pp. 1067-1097.

Croley, S.P. & Hanson, J.D. (1995). The nonpecuniary costs of accidents: pain-and-suffering damages in tort law. *Harvard Law Review, 108 (8)*, pp. 1785-1917.

Dohmen,T., Falk, A., Huffman, D. & Sunde, U. (2009), Homo reciprocans: survey evidence on behaviourial outcomes. *The Economic Journal*, 119 (March), pp. 592–612.

Faure, M.G. (1999), *Op de glijdende schaal van verzekerbare en onverzekerbare risico's. ESB, 84e jaargang*, nr. 4193, pp. D20-23.

Fehr, E. & Fischbacher, U. (2003). The nature of human altruism. *Nature*, 425, pp. 785-91.

Fehr, E. & Gachter, S. (1998), Reciprocity and economics: The economic implications of Homo reciprocans. *European Economic Review*, 42; pp. 845-59.

Feldman, H.L. (1997), Harm and money: against the insurance theory of tort Compensation, 75 *Tex. L. REV*. pp. 1567-1604.

Fischbacher, U. & Utikal, V. (2010). *On the acceptance of apologies*. Working paper no 53, June 2010. Research Paper Series Thurgau Institute of Economics and Department of Economics at the University of Konstanz.

Frech, H.E. (1994), State-dependent utility and the tort system as insurance: strict liability versus negligence. *International Review of Law and Economics*, 14, pp. 261-271.

Friedman, D. (1982). What is 'fair compensation' for death or injury? International Review of Law and Economics, 2, p. 81-93.

Huver, R.M.E., van Wees, K.A.P.C., Akermans, A.J. & Elbers, N.A. (2007). Slachtoffers en aansprakelijkheid. Een onderzoek naar behoeften, verwachtingen en ervaringen van slachtoffers en hun naasten met betrekking tot het civiele aansprakelijkheidsrecht. Deel I, Terreinverkenning. Den Haag: WODC.

Kaplow, L. & Shavell, S. (2002), Economic Analysis of Law. In A.J. Auerbach and M. Feldstein, eds, Handbook of Public Economics, vol. 3, pp. 1661–1784. Elsevier; The Netherlands.

King, J. H. (2004). Pain and suffering, noneconomic damages, and the goals of tort law. *S.M.U.* L. Rev. 18, p. 163-210.

Lindenbergh, S.D. (2008), *Smartengeld, tien jaar later*. Deventer: Kluwer.

Manning, R.L. (1994). Changing Rules in Tort Law and the Market for Childhood Vaccines. 37 *Journal of Law and Economics*, 247-275.

Miller, D.T., (2001), Disrespect and experience of injustice, Annual Review of Psychology, 52, pp. 527-53.

O'Connell, M. (2003). Criminal Injuries Compensation. Revisiting the rationale for state funded compensation for crime victims. Paper presented at the Innovation: Promising Practices for Victims and Witnesses in the Criminal Justice System – A National Conference, Canberra, 23 – 24 June, 2003.

Polinksy, A. M. & Shavell, S. (1998), Punitive damages an economic analysis. *Harvard Law Review*, 111(4), pp. 869-962.

Relis, T. (2006). Civil litigation from litigants' perspectives: what we know and what we don't know about the litigation experience of individual litigants. *Studies in Law, Politics and Society, 25*, p. 151–212.

Shavell, S. (2003). *Economic analysis of incident law.* NBER working paper nr. 9482; www.nber.org/papers/w9483. This paper contains the chapters on accident law from Shavell's book: Foundations of Economic analysis of law. Cambridge, Massachusetts: Harvard University Press, 2003.

Tyler, T. R. & Thorisdottir, H. (2004), A psychological perspective on compensation for harm: Examining the September 11th Victim Compensation Fund. *DePaul Law Review*, 53, pp. 355-391.

Vandenberghe, A.M.I.B. (2010). Non-Discrimination in the common principles of European contract law, in *Economic Analysis of the DCFR*, Larouch, P. , e.a., (Eds.), pp., 45-63, Munich: Sellier.

Verburg, G.J.M. (2009), *Vaststelling van smartengeld*. Deventer: Kluwer.

Viscusi, W.K. (2000), Misuses and proper uses of hedonic values of life, *Journal of Forensic Economics*, 13, pp. 111–125.

Viscusi, W.K. (1996), pain and suffering: damages in search of a sounder rationale, *Michigan Law & Policy Review*, 1, pp. 141–167.

Viscusi, W.K. (1996), pain and suffering: damages in search of a sounder rationale, Michigan Law & Policy Review, 1, pp. 141–167.

How to compensate a victim's losses? An economic perspective

By J.D.W.E. Mulder[6]

This chapter is an adaptation from Mulder, J.D.W.E. (2009), How do we compensate a victim's losses? An economic perspective. International Review of Victimology. Vol. 16, pp. 67–87.

Abstract

Compensatory damages awarded in court are intended to make victims 'whole again'. This raises the question how one could actually accomplish the goal of 'making whole' by means of financial compensation. This paper provides an overview of the theories used by the economists that have dealt with this question. Subsequently, the paper purports a new perspective on compensation by explaining how victims could be compensated by both financial and non-financial forms of compensation.

Introduction

'Lotto rapist' Iorworth Hoare had no money when he was jailed for life in 1989 for the attempted rape of Mrs. A (who cannot be named for legal reasons). Yet, shortly before being freed on parole Hoare's financial situation changed dramatically: he won £7 million after buying a lottery ticket during his day release from prison. At the time of Hoare's imprisonment, Mrs. A had not sued for damages because she had been told Hoare's lack of funds would have made it worthless (Reuters, 2007). Yet now that Hoare is a free man and a millionaire, Mrs. A wants him to pay for her psychiatric injury as, according to her, the attempted rape damaged her self-esteem and ruined her life (BBC, 2007; BBC, 2008).[7]

---

6 Ms. Mulder is grateful for the extensive comments by Eric van Damme, along with comments from Marc Groenhuijsen, Joanna Shapland and two anonymous referees.

7 There were many legal hurdles for Mrs. A to take before she could start a civil case against Mr. Hoare. When Hoare was released from jail in 2004, a legal limit of six years prevented her from suing him straightaway as the crime had taken place 16 years before. Mrs. A had to take her case up to the Law Lords (the highest legal court in the United Kingdom) who ruled, in the beginning of 2008, that the legal limit that kept Mrs. A from suing is unfair (Guardian Unlimited, 2008). Mrs. A, however, had to await a decision of the High Court on her particular case to see whether she was actually allowed to sue. In July 2008, four years after she made her first attempt to file a case against Hoare, the court cleared the final legal hurdle and allowed Mrs. A to claim compensation (BBC, 2008). *Update: in March 2009 Mrs A and Hoare reached an out-of-court settlement. All the money from that settlement was given to charity. In 2012 Shirley Woodman was made a Member of the Most Excellent Order of the British Empire (MBE) and, therefore, lifted her anonymity (see BBC News, January

Compensatory damages, like Mrs. A is claiming, are intended to return victims of tortuous acts as closely as possible to the condition they were in before the loss, or to make them 'whole again' (King, 2004, p. 165).[8] But what is it that could make Mrs. A as well off as she was before the rape? Should Hoare be required to pay her £100.000? Or should he pay her at least £1 million?

The central topic of this paper is how to compensate victims for their losses. I will expound the framework that is used by economic scholars to analyze the effects of compensation. The starting point within this framework is a victim's well-being, expressed in terms of utility. Since an individual's well-being is negatively affected by the sustainment of a loss, victims experience less utility from life and wealth than they did before a crime or accident. Making victims whole, therefore, implies compensating the utility they lost. According to renowned economists, there is just one method to determine the amount of compensatory damages that should be awarded in court: assessing the amount of first-party insurance that a victim would have bought voluntarily (on an actuarially fair basis) in a world without tort law (Viscusi, 1996, p. 153; Shavell, 2003, ch. 5, p. 10).

This 'theory of insurance' provides straightforward conclusions. It shows, for example, how people only wish to buy insurance against economic losses (losses that have substitutes or that can be repaired). Therefore, according to insurance theory, the only losses that should be awarded compensation in court are those of the economic kind. In other words, no compensation should be granted for non-economic losses (pain and suffering). Consequently, whether or not there exists an amount of financial compensation that could make Mrs. A whole again, lotto-rapist Hoare should not be forced to turn over (some of) his money to Mrs. A, not now nor twenty years ago.

Many legal and economic scholars share the conclusion that non-economic losses should not be compensated in court.[9] This paper will argue, however, that insurance theory falls short in determining the appropriate amount of damages when it comes to non-economic losses, due to its focus on financial compensation. It will do so by referring to several studies that have shown how "litigants are propelled into litigation as a result of not only material but also psychological and emotional needs to alleviate the effects of distressing experiences" (Relis, 2006, p. 193; see Huver et al., 2007 for similar conclusions). In other words, the focus of insurance theory, and most legal

3th, 2012; New Year Honours: Leeds lottery rapist victim made MBE, http://www.bbc.co.uk/news/uk-england-leeds-16396083)

8 This is a leading principle in various countries, like for instance the United States, the United Kingdom, Germany and the Netherlands (See Verburg, 2009; Lindenbergh, 2008).

9 Many scholars seem to oppose compensation of non-economic losses out of resentment of the large amounts of financial compensation awarded in the United States for pain and suffering; Louis Jaffe, for instance, already wrote in 1953 about the "parasitic damages" for pain and suffering (p. 223).

advisors (Relis, 2007), on financial compensation as the sole method to make victims 'whole again', seems to be an over-simplified view on victims' needs. This is particularly true as extensive research on procedural fairness has shown how non-monetary matters like being able to ask questions and to experience polite and respectful treatment, contribute to an individual's well-being, irrespective of instrumental outcomes like financial compensation (Frey et al., 2004, p. 381).

The present paper shows how the economic framework of well-being is very well suited to analyze both financial and other forms of compensation, and it will show how they are closely related. Yet, it is not possible to provide a clear, practical recommendation on the amount of compensatory damages that should be awarded in court, nor on what kind of non-financial forms of compensation should be provided. The reason why it is impossible to do so is that, although compensatory damages have intended to make victims whole again for many years, it is still unknown how economic and non-economic forms of compensation actually work and how they are interrelated. For instance, we do not know yet how much compensation is needed to make a victim whole again,[10] and how this amount could be lowered in case of acknowledgement or respectful treatment.

The paper is structured as follows; first of all it shall explain how an individual's well-being is expressed in terms of utility and how utility can be used to assess the amount of compensation that is needed to make a victim whole again. Next, shall be described what kind of role insurance theory plays in determining court compensation and what this theory entails. After this it will be shown how a tort process affects an individual's utility just like a tort outcome does, and finally the paper will expound how non-financial forms of compensation affect the amount of financial compensation, and how it, therefore, seems no longer accurate to disregard this type of utility when it comes to determining court compensation.

1. Making whole

Victims who incur losses due to the tortuous acts of others can claim compensation for their losses through tort (civil) law procedures.[11] Such

10 As shown in special edition 14(2) of this journal, several studies have strived to determine the financial value of crime's 'intangible' consequences. One might think that these financial values are good indicators of the compensatory damages that could make victims whole again. However, such values have little to do with *compensation* of non-economic losses, as they are mere *conversions*. Hence, the results of studies like the ones mentioned in the special edition, do not provide any guidance when it comes to compensation of pain and suffering.

11 In some countries it is possible for victims of crime to claim compensation during a criminal trial as well. In the Netherlands, for example, a victim's civil suit can be brought into the criminal procedure under condition that it concerns a simple claim (more complex cases are

compensatory damages are intended to "return the plaintiff as closely as possible to his or her condition before the wrongful act" and "make the plaintiff whole" (King, 2004, p. 165).[12] Legal instructions, however, provide very little guidance to ascertain the award of damages that could make a victim 'whole' again (Vicusi & Born, 2005, p. 25; Viscusi, 2003, p. 2). Jurors in the United States, for example, are instructed "that the object of an award of damages is to place the plaintiff, as far as money can do, in the situation he would have occupied if the wrong had not been committed" (Douthwaite, 1988, p.3, as cited by Shuman, 1994). But how can a victim be put back in the ex ante situation? Renowned economic scholars have tried to answer this question and in the following section their analysis shall be purported.

1.1. *A victim's well-being*

In economics, the concept of utility is used to analyze the level of well-being that an individual person experiences. Although a person's well-being depends on many different factors, utility is usually related to wealth. To start with, we do so as well: the amount of utility that individual i experiences is denoted by Ui(W) and Figure 1 on the next page shows graphically how a person gets more satisfied as his wealth increases.

Before we can see how one's utility is affected by losses, it is of importance to distinguish economic losses from non-economic losses (pain and suffering).[13] Economic losses are those incurred by the loss of money and of goods for which substitutes can be bought (Shavell, 2003, ch. 4, p. 12). Examples are a stolen car or wallet, thorn clothes and lost income. Pain and suffering, on the other hand, is intangible. In other words: for non-economic losses like physiological pain, mental anguish, distress, loss of enjoyment of life, and psychological effects of disfigurement, no market substitutes are available, nor can they be repaired (King, 2004, p. 164).14 For some losses, like the theft of an 18th century painting, it is disputable whether it is an economic or a non-economic loss. Yet as a first approximation, one could state that what

only dealt with by the civil court). Since compensation is intended to make a victim whole, whether it is awarded during a civil or a criminal case, the analysis purported in this article is applicable to compensation awarded during both civil and criminal procedures.

12 See footnote 2.

13 Many different terms are used to represent damages, for example: economic-damages, loss, compensation, award, deterrence value, value of life, hedonic damages, pecuniary damages, and monetary damages (Schieren, 1998, p. 37-8). Although they are often used as synonyms, I would like to stress that these terms *can* represent different concepts (e.g. Sunstein, 2007).

14 As Cook & Graham (1977, p. 144) explain: there are no markets for continuing sources of utility, such as good health, the life of a friend, or freedom of speech. Although an individual may be able to assess the monetary value of such "assets" (and may indeed be faced with decisions that in effect require such assessments), his personal valuation is not tied to any market price.

distinguishes an economic loss from a non-economic one is the possibility to calculate a market price. Psychiatric medical expenses, for example, could be defined as an economic loss as the market value of these services is determined by psychiatrists every day, while emotional losses like anxiety and grieve are non-economic as their value is not tied to any market price.

Figure 1: utility curve

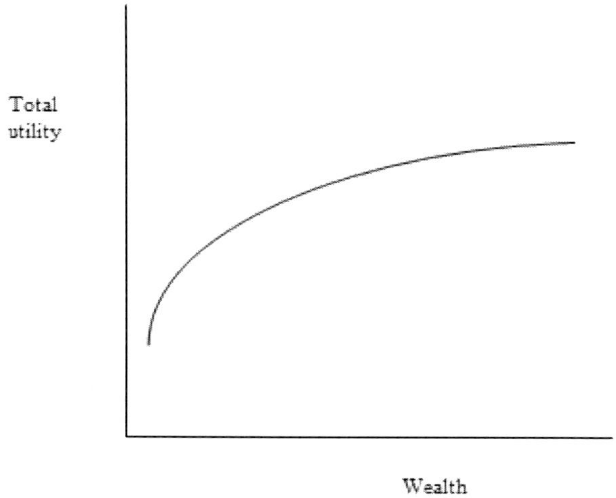

1.2. *How losses affect one's well-being*

Imagine there is a person i, and that this person's car becomes damaged in a traffic accident. Repairing the damage will cost i an amount of money equal to D. Due to these costs, i's wealth (W) will decrease to W-D. Consequently, i's utility will decrease from $U_i(W)$ in situation A (before the accident), to $U_i(W\text{-}D)$ in situation B (after the accident), as graphically shown in Figure 2.

To return individual i as closely as possible to the situation before the accident, its utility needs to be returned to the level of $U_i(W)$. The question, therefore, is: how much compensatory damages (C) should be awarded in court so that i will experience $U_i(W)$ again? In other words, which amount of C will make i as good as he was before the accident, so that:

$$U_i(W) = U_i(W-D+C)$$

The answer to this question is not that difficult to provide. After all, if compensation C equals i's incurred loss D, i will shift back from point B to A. Hence, when compensation is set equal to the cost of i's car restoration, i will be made whole again. This conclusion is illustrative for all types of economic losses; full compensation of incurred damages, valued by the cost of repair or replacement, will bring a victim back to his or her initial level of utility (Cook & Graham, 1977).

Figure 2: Economic losses (D) cause a downward shift on the utility curve

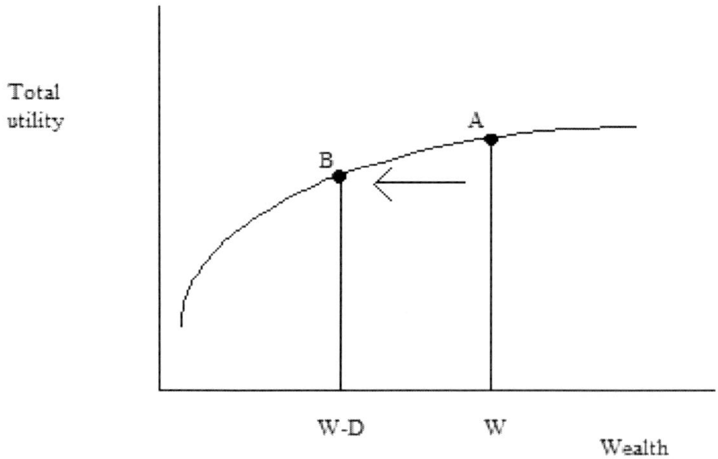

Now imagine that individual i incurs a non-economic loss instead of an economic one. In order to assess the impact of this loss on i's well-being, the utility function Ui(W) has to be extended with a factor that symbolises i's emotional state (E). After all, a non-economic loss is not a matter of wealth but of emotions. The utility function, therefore, becomes: $U_i(W, E)$. Like an increase in wealth (W), improvement of individual i's emotional state (E) has a positive effect on his utility: the better his emotional state, the more utility he will experience. This positive effect is represented by an upward shift of the utility curve (Cook & Graham, 1977), as shown in Figure 3 by a shift from Uo to U1. In case of non-economic losses the opposite occurs; i's utility curve drops to a lower level, from Uo to U1', making individual i, all things considered, less well off than before (Cooter, 1989; Geistfeld, 1995).

A person who might have been affected in this way may well be rape victim Mrs. A, whose case was described in the introduction. Mrs. A claims her life is ruined after the attack of Iorworth Hoare (BBC, 2007), and as she does not claim any economic damages, it seems reasonable to assume that the incident shifted Mrs. A's utility curve downwards, as shown in Figure 3, causing everything in her life to be less valuable than before.

Figure 3: Utility curve moves vertically with an increase/decrease of ones emotional state

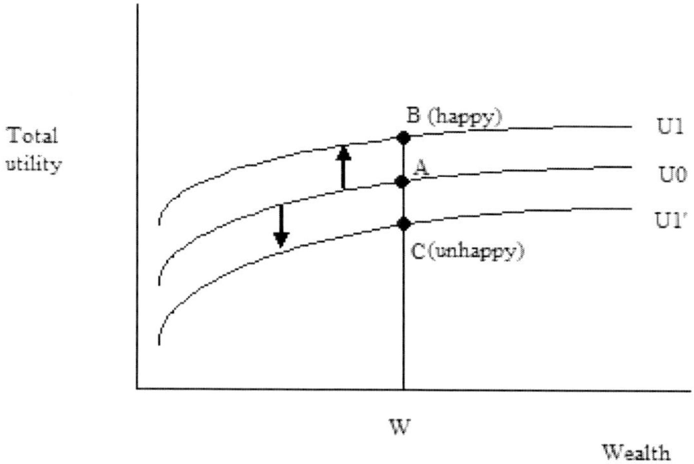

The state in which a victim ends up after sustaining non-economic loss, we denote by E', and his utility level, consequently, by $U_i(W, E')$. The amount of utility that i loses due to the pain and suffering he incurred, is equal to the difference between his utility before the incident, $U_i(W, E)$, and that after the incident, $U_i(W, E')$. To return individual i as closely as possible to his situation before the incident, this difference in utility needs to be compensated, so that:

$$U_i(W, E) = U_i(W+C, E')$$

This brings us to the question whether there is an amount of *financial* compensation that could offset an *emotional* loss. And if so, how could we determine the appropriate amount? Contrary to the loss of economic commodities, it is not possible to buy a bottle of positive emotions or to hire someone to repair a victim's grief or fear. Hence, compensation cannot be assessed with the use of market prices. Several methods are suggested to overcome this lack of data.[15] According to renowned economists, however,

[15] To overcome the lack of market data, it has been suggested to simply ask victims how much financial compensation they would need in order to overcome their loss. Unfortunately, extensive research has shown how such 'stated preferences' lead to unreliable conclusions; people tend to exaggerate their loss (rent seeking) on the one hand, and to give socially acceptable answers on the other (e.g. Diamond & Hausman, 1994; Hammitt and Graham, 1999, show how people are insensitive to changes in risk). An approach that does not lead to the desired estimates either, is the one used by some courts in the United States, namely extracting value of life numbers (Viscusi, 2000a). The value of life can be constructed by examining how much individuals are willing to pay to avoid a certain risk (WTP) or how much compensation they need to accept a certain risk (WTA). Yet, all that this number indicates is that people are willing to trade off small risks of death against money. The value does not imply that people are willing to trade their life for $5 million or so, nor that victims

there is only one appropriate method to assess court compensation: identifying the amount of first-party insurance that would have been bought voluntarily (on an actuarially fair basis) in a world without tort laws (Viscusi, 2000, p. 116; Shavell, 2003, ch. 5, p. 10). This 'theory of insurance' shall be explained in the next paragraph.

2. Theory of insurance

In order to assess the amount of compensation that should be awarded in court, many economists have used the thought experiment of how much insurance coverage a victim would have chosen to provide *after* the accident, if offered the opportunity to buy such insurance on an actuarially fair basis *before* the accident (Viscusi, 2003, p. 2-3).[16]In this section we shall do the same; but first I will explain more about the purchase of insurance.

When individual i decides to buy an actuarially fair first-party insurance policy, i chooses to incur a certain but relatively small loss now (the cost of the insurance premium) in order to avoid an uncertain but relatively substantial loss in the future (the full cost of an incident). Yet, individual i will only choose to buy such a policy when he will value an extra dollar more in the post-accident situation than he does in the pre-accident situation (Shavell, 2003, ch. 5, p. 9-10). Let me explain: Figures 1-3 showed us the utility curve: unmistakeably this curve is not a straight line but a concave one. This particular characteristic of the utility curve indicates how, although utility increases as wealth grows, there is a point from where individual i values every extra dollar less than the dollars he already possesses. Put differently; the value of an extra dollar decreases as wealth increases. This phenomenon is what economists call 'decreasing marginal utility of wealth': the marginal utility of a dollar, symbolized by $mU_i(W)$, decreases as wealth increases. As said, by buying insurance, individual i shifts money from the pre-accident state A to the post-accident state B, clearly i will only do so when he values an extra dollar more in B than he does in A. How this works out for the compensation of economic and non-economic losses respectively will be explained in the upcoming sections.

---

who state that they enjoy life after the incident only half as much as before, should be awarded $2.5 million. Like Viscusi (2000, p. 115-6) states: the value-of-life estimates are not a retrospective measure of compensation.

16 In actuarially fair markets, premiums are equal to expected benefit payments. This could only occur if insurance was costless to administer, losses were statistically independent, there was no moral hazard or adverse selection, and if insurance markets were perfectly competitive. The reason for assuming actuarially fair markets is explained by Frech (1994, p. 263): the assumption of insurance on an actually fair basis is made to rule out moral hazard and adverse selection; by doing so, the focus lies on risk spreading and consequently, the condition for efficient insurance is that the marginal utility of wealth with and without an accident are equal.

2.1. *Insurance of economic losses*

Imagine again that individual i's car becomes damaged in a traffic accident. As shown in Figure 4, this economic loss D reduces i's wealth and thus his utility. Knowing this in the ex ante situation, will i choose to buy insurance to compensate this loss?

Due to his damaged car, individual i will move from pre-accident state A to post-accident state B on the utility curve, as his utility drops from $U_i(W)$ to $U_i(W\text{-}D)$ (see Figure 4). As explained, marginal utility of wealth is higher in B than it is in A: $mU_i(W) < mU_i(W\text{-}D)$. Assuming i can oversee this wealth impacting effect up front, i knows he will value an extra dollar more in point B than he does in A, and therefore prefers to shift money from A to B, up until the point where marginal utility of money in both states are equalized (Arrow, 1971). As explained, he can do so by buying an insurance policy. Yet, insurance is costly. Assuming it is actuarially fair, i will have to pay an insurance premium, X, that equals the expected benefits times the chance of incurring the corresponding losses. Due to this premium, X, i's initial level of wealth will drop from W to W-X.

Figure 4: optimal level of insurance and compensation in case of economic losses

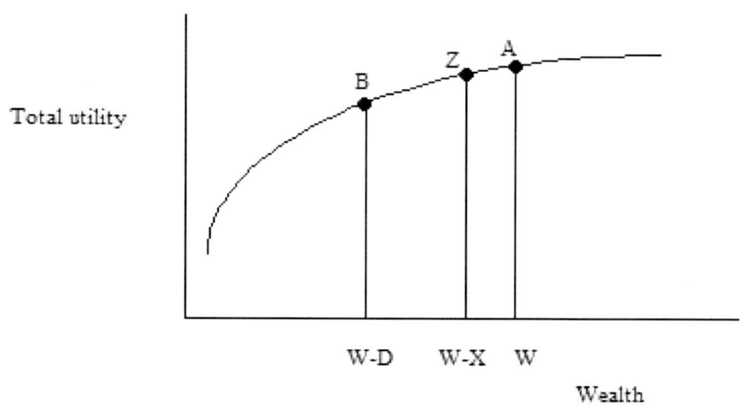

Given that *full insurance* is what equals marginal utility in both states of the world,[17] i will experience income level W-X and the corresponding utility level of $U_i(W\text{-}X)$ irrespective of whether an accident occurs (Viscusi, 1996, p. 148). In other words, buying insurance makes i *indifferent* between the two states

[17] As said, the insurance premium (X) equals the expected benefits (B) times the chance of incurring the corresponding loss (p): X = pC. If individual i buys insurance, he faces two possible situations: one with chance 1-p in which he will have no accident and experiences Ui(W-pB), and one with chance p in which he will have an accident, receives insurance payment and, thus, experiences Ui(W-pB-D+C). In order to maximize his expected utility (MaxB {pU(W-pB-D+C)+(1-p)U(W-pB)}), and equal marginal utility in both states, i will buy full insurance (B=D).

of the world that he is facing, as represented by point Z in Figure 4.

So the question whether i will choose to buy insurance can be answered positively. And as *full insurance* is the amount of insurance that individual i would buy voluntarily (on an actuarially fair basis), we can conclude that *full compensation* is the appropriate amount to award in court in case of economic losses. After all, the theory of insurance tells us that compensation awarded in court should equal the amount of insurance bought voluntarily. So in the case of economic losses, the amount of compensation (C) should equal that of incurred losses D (C=D) (Viscusi, 2008, p. 2-3). As we saw in the previous section, this level of compensation will make i whole again as well.

2.2. *Insurance of non-economic losses*

Would person i be willing to buy (full) insurance against non-economic losses too? As explained earlier, when i incurs pain and suffering, he will not shift to another position on his utility curve, but his utility curve itself will shift downwards (as shown in Figure 5). How does this affect his demand for insurance?

As Figure 5 shows, i's utility level at post-accident point B is lower than it is at pre-accident point A, as $U_i(W, E) > U_i(W, E')$, implying that i is worse off after the accident than he was before the accident. The marginal utility of money, however, is the same in both states of the world ($mU_i(W, E) = mU_i(W, E')$). Consequently, there is no incentive for i to shift dollars from the pre-accident state to the post-accident and thus no motive to buy insurance. Moreover, one could pose that an uninsured person facing pain and suffering is already optimally insured (because marginal utility of wealth is the same whether or not the loss occurs) (Calfee & Rubin, 1992, p. 375). As a result, the level of insurance that an individual would buy voluntarily in case of non-economic damages is zero. Hence, according to insurance theory, the level of compensation awarded in court should equal zero as well.

Figure 5: Optimal insurance level and compensation in case of non-economic losses

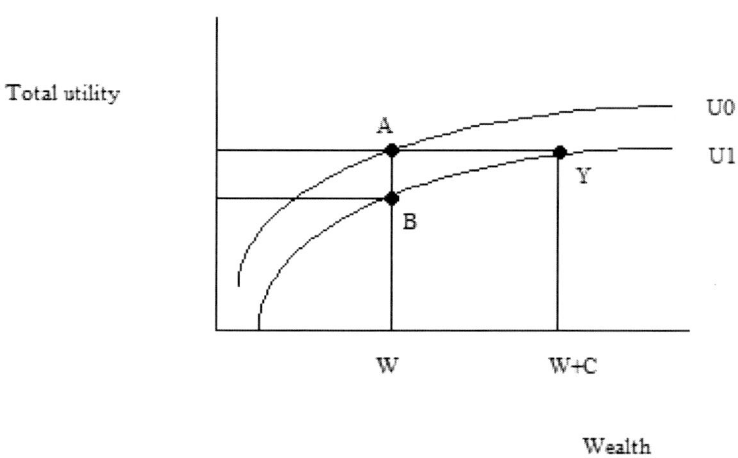

Nevertheless, there is an amount of compensation that would bring individual i back to his pre-accident level of utility, as can be seen in Figure 5. By awarding amount C, i would shift from point B on U_1 to Y on U_1 and as a consequence, individual i would be made 'whole again' (as $U_i(W, E) = U_i(W+C,E')$). However, "the goal of full compensation to victims of violent crime or accidents that result in injury or death is not compatible with economic efficiency" (Cook & Graham, 1977, p. 151), as it leads to excessive *overinsurance*. After all, insurance theory shows how individuals wish to buy no insurance at all and awarding them any compensation would thus lead to 'overinsurance'. So, although there is an amount that could make a victim whole again, it is stated that courts should not award any compensation for pain and suffering (Viscusi, 2008, p. 9-10).

In sum, we can conclude that the amount of damages that could make a victim whole again in case of economic losses is the same amount that people would be willing to buy insurance for, and therefore, full compensation is what should be awarded in court. For non-economic losses, on the other hand, people are not willing to buy insurance for the amount that could make them whole again. Moreover, they do not want to buy any insurance against non-economic losses at all. Hence, insurance theory states that the amount of damages that should be awarded in court for this type of losses is equal to zero.

The insurance-based-analysis, as described in this section, is frequently used by economists to assess compensatory damages. The conclusions seem firm and straightforward. It is important to mention, however, that the assumptions, on which this analysis is based, are heavily debated. Why this is, will be explained in the next paragraph.

2.3. *Discussion on demand for pain and suffering insurance*

Insurance theory assumes that non-economic damages have no effect on one's marginal utility of wealth, and that therefore, neither insurance nor court compensation is needed. There is a lively debate, however, on a person's actual demand for insurance against pain and suffering and thus, on the levels of compensation that should be awarded in court. Some scholars say, for instance, that pain and suffering has no effect on the marginal utility of wealth, in line with the theory of insurance. Others state that non-economic damages have a positive effect; an often cited example is that of an individual who is crippled by an accident and who might need additional money, even after being compensated for medical expenses and forgone income, because of a need to obtain household help, special transportation services and the like (Shavell, 2003, ch. 5, p. 9). This line of reasoning, however, does not support the hypothesis that pain and suffering increases the need for money since the types of consumption items mentioned are generally included as part of rehabilitation package, and they need not be considered under the pain and suffering component of an award (Viscusi, 1993, p. 179). There is also a group of scholars who claim that pain and suffering has a negative effect on the need for money (e.g. Friedman, 1982). Death, for instance, reduces utility drastically, without heirs even to zero (Schwartz, 1988, p. 364; Arlen, 2000; Shavell, 2003, ch. 5, p. 9). However, as Viscusi (1993, p. 179) points out, one cannot generalize to all nonfatal injuries such as disabilities and conclude that the marginal utility of income has been diminished. Overall, we can state that there is no theoretical consensus. Is there empirical evidence then?

To date, only a few studies have tried to empirically examine the effects of pain and suffering on the marginal utility of wealth. Unfortunately, their conclusions are antipodal as well. The renowned article of Viscusi & Evans (1991), for instance, suggests that serious on-the-job injuries may reduce the victim's marginal utility of wealth, which favors the hypothesis that consumers do not wish to buy insurance.[18] Other studies, however, show how consumers do prefer insurance for certain kinds of pain and suffering injuries (Calfee & Winston, 1993; Avraham, 2005), implying that non-economic losses do increase the need for money. In fact, some forms of insurance that cover pain and suffering are actually sold (Croley & Hanson, 1995).

All and all, there is no solid and conclusive proof for the effects of non-economic losses on marginal utility, neither theoretically or empirically. This implies that it is not certain how non-economic losses change one's utility curve. Consequently, we can conclude that it is not clear whether the curves graphed in Figure 1-5, which are often used within economic literature to show the effects of losses on well-being, represent the actual effects that victims experience. One thing, however, is undisputed. People almost never buy insurance against pain and suffering (although the explanations for the non-existence of a market for pain and suffering insurance differ considerably).[19] This empirical fact is for most scholars reason to stick to the

---

[18] Moreover, the study of Viscusi & Evans provides evidence for the hypothesis of Friedman (1982) that pain and suffering decreases the marginal utility of money and that, therefore, it would be better to compensate victims ex ante (see Friedman, 1982 for more information).

[19] According to several scholars, people would be willing to buy insurance (See for example; Croley & Hanson, 1995; Avraham, 2003, 2005 & 2006 and Pryor, 1993) but is it impossible to do so because of market failure. Moral hazard, for example, would keep insurance companies from selling non-economic insurance (Croley & Hanson, 1995, p. 1848-51). Two other often mentioned constraints are 1) consumers wouldn't be competent to assess the risks they run and their possible consequences (Avraham, 2005, p. 955; Pryor, 1993) and 2) strong social norms would prohibit the assignment of a monetary value to items not normally traded in the marketplace (Croley & Hanson, 1995, p. 1851-3). Although these constraints may seem valid, they do not explain the fact why people do buy insurance against economic loss but (almost) never against non-economic harm. After all, moral hazard and information problems are also present in the assessment of economic risks, and how can it be that social norms prohibit consumers to buy insurance against pain and suffering but not

theory that "people prefer not to insure against 'mental' losses, because they almost never do insure against them" (Schwartz, 1988, p. 365). The general consensus, therefore, seems to be that pain and suffering should not be compensated in court because it leads to (excessive) overinsurance (e.g. Arlen, 2000; Shavell, 2003; Kaplow & Shavell, 2002; Viscusi, 2008; Viscusi, 2000 and Viscusi, 1996).[20]

3. Other means to compensation

The previous sections show how there is a clear focus on financial compensation when it comes to making victims whole again. In itself, this focus follows logically from the fact that all what victims can claim, is financial compensation. Several studies, however, have shown that it is rather deceiving to think that plaintiffs only care about financial compensation. When asked about their objectives, plaintiffs mention several goals, and most of them are not financial. The upcoming paragraphs, will explain what these objectives are and why they are important factors in the compensation discussion.

3.1. Why plaintiffs go to court

It may seem as though plaintiffs only care about the consequences of a trial and that their only concern is receiving as much financial compensation as possible. Recent studies on litigants' goals and experiences, however, shows that "litigants are propelled into litigation as a result of not only material but also psychological and emotional needs to alleviate the effects of distressing experiences" (Relis, 2006, p. 193; see Huver et al., 2007 for similar conclusions). Emotional needs even seem to be the cardinal goals of litigants in tort, divorce, injury and small claims cases (Relis, 2007, p. 19-20). Moreover, a recent study with the pronounced title "it is not about the money", shows how plaintiffs in medical malpractice cases, when asked about their motives, fail to mention financial compensation as an objective at all, unless probed. Instead, plaintiffs recurrently repeat a number of non-fiscal, extra-legal objectives for their litigation, for example, dignity and respect after the injury, inability to be heard otherwise, refusal to listen, dismissal and victim blaming (Relis, 2007, p.21). These findings are in line with those of other studies; prevention of similar occurrences, acknowledgement, admission that something had gone wrong and answers, are very important objectives for litigants. Compensation, on the other hand, seems to be one of the less important goals (Relis, 2007, p. 21-3).

to sue for compensation in court?

[20] From an insurance perspective it is only reasonable to award compensation for pain and suffering on grounds of deterrence. In that case, however, awarded compensation should be paid to the state, since payment to the victim will lead to (excessive) overinsurance (Kaplow & Shavell, 2002, p. 8).

So it seems that going to court entails more for plaintiffs than just a means to receive financial compensation. But does this imply that there are others means to compensate a victim's losses besides financial compensation?

3.2. *Procedural utility*

The renowned works on procedural fairness of Thibaut & Walker and Lind & Tyler, and others following in their tradition, show how plaintiffs do not only care about the outcome of a trial, but also care deeply about the process by which conflicts are resolved and decisions are made, even when outcomes are unfavourable or the process they desire is slow or costly (MacCoun, 2005). In other words, plaintiffs do not only care about the outcome of a procedure, they also care about the procedures through which outcomes are generated. Nobel laureate Amartya Sen (1995, 1997) was the first economist to acknowledge the beneficial effects of processes. Following in his footsteps, Frey et al. (2004) 'translated' the concept of procedural fairness into 'procedural utility'. The term procedural utility implies that people value certain procedures for obtaining outcomes more than other procedures (Frey et al., 2004). But why would people prefer one procedure over the other while they both lead to the same outcome?

According to Frey et al. (2004, p. 380) "procedural utility emerges because people have a 'sense of self'", in other words, procedural utility exists because people care about how they perceive themselves as human beings and how they are perceived by others. Important information about the self is provided by procedures. Specifically, they address innate psychological needs of self-determination (Frey et al., 2004, p. 380). Three such needs are proven to be essential: autonomy, relatedness, and competence. The need for autonomy encompasses the desire to self-organize one's own actions. The need for relatedness refers to the desire to feel connected to others in love and care, and to be treated as a respected group member within social groups. The third need, that for competence, reflects the propensity to control the environment and to see oneself as capable and effective (Frey et al. 2004, p. 380). Different procedures can be expected to support these three needs differently; procedures therefore contribute to an individual's well-being irrespective of instrumental outcomes (Frey et al., 2004, p. 381).

3.3. *How does this relate to insurance theory?*

If one takes procedural utility into account, is insurance theory then still an appropriate tool to assess court compensation? Unmistakably, the procedure of a tort case differs from that of a first-party insurance payment. But will these different procedures affect the utility that victims derive from financial compensation? Since plaintiffs in a tort case have the opportunity to participate, to tell one's story, to experience polite and respectful treatment and to receive consideration to their needs and concerns, the answer to this question seems positive. After all, according to scholars working on the topic of procedural fairness, these opportunities are precisely what make plaintiffs evaluate their standing and status as favorable (Tyler, 2006, p. 374). Compensation through insurance, on the other hand, provides none of such opportunities: filling in a few forms is generally all one has (and can) to do to get losses reimbursed. Hence, it seems doubtful that filing an insurance claim supports any of the mentioned psychological needs of self-determination.

Due to the differences in process characteristics and their subsequent effect on a victim's psychological needs, one could state that victims gain more well-being from receiving the same amount of financial compensation through a tort law procedure than from a first-party insurance payment. Furthermore, the concept of procedural utility and the psychological needs it refers to, are strikingly in line with the earlier described motives of plaintiffs' to start a law suit. Telling one's story, dignity and respect after the injury, being heard, acknowledgement, admission that something had gone wrong, and answers to one's questions; all goals that contribute to the 'sense of self'. And none of them can be accomplished through first-party insurance. The same is true for prevention of similar occurrences, and, not in the least, for making the offender responsible for the consequences of his or her actions; several studies have shown how victims of crime have a strong preference for compensation directly by the offender, rather than the state for instance, due to the offender's responsibility for the incurred harm (Shapland, Willmore & Duff, 1986; Huver, 2007, p. 39; Cobley, 1998, p. 222).

Due to the different ways in which court procedures support a person's psychological need of self-determination, it seems that receiving financial compensation through court procedures restores a victim's well-being in two distinct ways, namely: financial and non-financial. As plaintiffs themselves state that the non-financial forms of compensation are more important to them than the economic ones, it seems that insurance theory falls short in determining what is needed to 'return the plaintiff as closely as possible to his or her condition before the wrongful act'. After all, it assumes that buying insurance is a substitute for going to court, while buying insurance does not seem to support a 'sense of self' in any way.

The economic framework of utility, however, can be used to analyze the different effects of several sorts of compensation. What happens if one uses this framework, shall be explained in the next paragraph.

3.4. Taking non-economic factors into account

To show how non-economic factors affect a person's well-being, we continue the line of reasoning set out in the first section of this paper. We use utility function $U_i(W, E)$, to make sure that we analyze not only wealth related effects, but also those related to alterations in i's emotional state. As shown earlier, an improvement of individual i's emotional state (E) has a positive effect on his utility: the better his emotional state, the more utility he will experience. So when person i experiences procedural utility during a court case, because he feels acknowledged as a victim for, or because his questions are being answered, his well-being will improve, and subsequently, his utility curve will shift upwards. Figure 6 shows this shift graphically: i goes from position B on utility curve U1, to position J on U2.

Figure 6: Effects of procedural utility on the amount of financial compensation needed to make a plaintiff whole again.

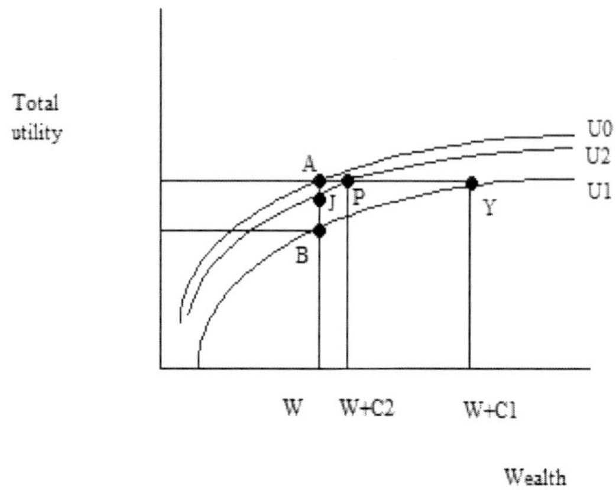

The amount of financial compensation that is needed to bring i from position J to one that is equal to his initial position, in other words: to make i whole again, is equal to C2. After all, as Figure 6 shows us, an amount of C2 will bring i to position P on U2, and there his level of utility will be the same as it was in initial position A on Uo.

The amount of compensatory damages C2 differs significantly from that of C_1 (C_1 being the amount needed to make i whole again when procedural utility is not taken into account). The difference between these amounts depends, of course, on the extent of the curve's shift upwards, but nonetheless, the difference shows how economic and non-economic forms of compensation are closely related: if one of them changes, the other one does as well. Since plaintiffs themselves state that non-financial objectives are of importance to them, and as these objectives affect their utility, we can conclude that non-financial forms of compensation can no longer be disregarded while determining the amount of compensation that should be awarded in court. Yet, as will be explained in the next paragraph, a lot of questions remain.

4. Questions that remain

As said earlier, jurors in the United States are instructed "that the object of an award of damages is to place the plaintiff, as far as money can do, in the situation he would have occupied if the wrong had not been committed" (Douthwaite, 1988, p.3, as cited by Shuman, 1994). Which award will do so? Figure 6 showed us how an amount of C2 in combination with non-financial forms of compensation will bring a victim back to his or her initial position. Of course the question then remains: how large should C2 be and moreover: what kind of non-financial compensation should be offered? Unfortunately, it is impossible to answer these questions as it is still unknown how non-financial forms of compensation actually affect one's utility. Moreover, we do not yet know how non-economic losses affect one's utility: as explained earlier there is a lively debate among scholars about the effects of non-economic losses. In other words, although thousands of victims sustain significant losses every day, and compensatory damages are intended to return them as closely as possible to their condition before the wrongful act, the literature on how to do so is still very limited. That is why I would like to urge that more research is needed to study the effects of losses on a person's well-being and how these effects could be reversed.

Summary

The central topic of this paper is how to compensate victims for their losses. Up till now, restoration of a victim's well being is seen as a pure financial matter. The insurance theory, which is used by most economists to determine the amount of money that should be awarded in court, for instance, only takes the financial effects of losses into account. The theory states that court compensation should equal the amount of insurance that people would have bought voluntarily on an actuarially fair basis. As people are only interested in buying insurance when a loss increases their marginal utility of wealth, and pain and suffering does not seem to have such an effect, it follows from this theory that courts should award zero compensation in case of non-economic losses. It is perceived as 'overinsurance' when victims do get compensation for pain and suffering, and therefore, seen as inefficient.

This paper shows how the theory of insurance falls short due to its focus on financial matters alone. Several studies have shown how plaintiffs do not go to court just to obtain financial compensation; they have several non-financial objectives as well. Telling one's story, dignity and respect after the injury, being heard, acknowledgement, admission that something had gone wrong, and answers to one's questions, are repeatedly mentioned by plaintiffs when asked about their motives for going to court. As none of these non-financial objectives could be obtained by buying insurance, it seems no longer correct to compare court compensation to buying insurance, as insurance theory does.

In this paper it is shown how non-financial forms of compensation can be used to restore a victim's well being, and how it, in combination with financial compensation, could be used to make a victim whole again. Unfortunately, however, is not yet possible to provide a clear, practical recommendation on the amount of compensatory damages that should be awarded in court, nor on what kind of non-financial forms of compensation should be provided. The reason why it is impossible to do so is that it is still unknown how economic and non-economic forms of compensation actually work and how they are interrelated. So although this paper shows how victims could theoretically be made whole again, much more research is needed to study how this could be done in practice.

References

Arlen, J. (2000). Tort Damages. In B. Bouckaert & G. De Geest (eds.), *Encyclopaedia of Law and Economics, vol. II*, pp. 682-734. Cheltenham: Edward Elgar.

Arrow, K. (1973). *Essays in the theory of risk bearing*. Chicago: Markham Publishing Co.

Avraham, R. (2003). *Pain-and-Suffering Damages in Tort Law: Revisiting the Theoretical Framework and the Empirical Data*. Michigan Law and Economics Research Paper No. 03-001; Northwestern Law & Econ Research Paper No. 03-03.

Avraham, R. (2005). Should pain-and-suffering damages be abolished from tort law? More experimental evidence. *University of Toronto Law Journal, 55*, p. 941-979.

Avraham, R. (2006). Putting a Price on Pain-and-Suffering Damages: A Critique of the Current Approaches and a Preliminary Proposal for Change. *Northwestern University Law Review, 100*, p. 81-120.

BBC, (2007). *Lords consider Lotto rapist case*. Retrieved November 11, 2007 from Website BBC News: http://news.bbc.co.uk/go/pr/fr/-/1/hi/uk/7072129.stm.

BBC, (2008). *Woman cleared to sue Lotto rapist*. Retrieved September 5, 2008 from Website BBC News: http://news.bbc.co.uk/go/pr/fr/-/1/hi/england/west_yorkshire/7495448.stm

Calfee, J.E. & Rubin, P.H. (1992). Some implications of damage payments for nonpecuniary losses. *Journal of Legal Studies, 21*, p. 371-412.

Calfee, J.E. & Winston, C. (1993). The consumer welfare effects of liability for pain and suffering: an exploratory analysis. *Brookings Papers on Economic Activity. Microeconomics, Vol. 1993* (1), pp. 133-196.

Cobley, C. (1998). Financial compensation for victims of child abuse. *Journal of Social Welfare and Family Law, 20(3),* p. 221-235.

Cook, P. J. & Graham, D.A. (1977). The demand for insurance and protection: the case of irreplaceable commodities. *The Quarterly Journal of Economics, 91 (1),* pp. 143-156.
Cooter, R. (1989). Towards a market in unmatured tort claims. *Virginia Law Review, 75,* p. 388-91.

Croley, S.P. & Hanson, J.D. (1995). The nonpecuniary costs of accidents: pain-and-suffering damages in tort law. *Harvard Law Review, 108(8),* p. 1785-1917).

Diamond, P.A. & Hausman, J.A. (1994). Contingent Valuation: Is Some Number better than No Number? *The Journal of Economic Perspectives, 8(4),* p. 45-64.

Frech, H.E. (1994), State-dependent utility and the tort system as insurance: strict liability versus negligence. *International Review of Law and Economic, 14,* p. 261-71.
Friedman, D. (1982). What is 'fair compensation' for death or injury? *International Review of Law and Economics, 2,* p. 81-93.

Friedman, D., (2000), *Law's order*. Princeton, New Jersey: Princeton University Press.

Frey, B.S., Benz, M. & Stutzer. A. (2004). Introducing procedural utility: not only what, but also how matters. Journal of Institutional and Theoretical Economics, 160(3), p. 377-401._

Guardian Unlimited, (2008). *Victim succeeds in claim against lottery-winning rapist.* Retrieved on January 30, 2008, from Guardian Unlimited website: http://www.guardian.co.uk/crime /article/0,,2249056,00.html

Geistfeld, M. (1995). Placing a price on pain and suffering: a method for helping juries determine tort damages for nonmonetary injuries. *California Law Review, 83,* p. 773-852.

Hammitt, J.K. & Graham, J.D. (1999). Willingness to Pay for Health Protection: Inadequate Sensitivity to Probability? *Journal of Risk and Uncertainty, 8,* p. 33-62.

Huver, R.M.E., van Wees, K.A.P.C., Akermans, A.J. & Elbers, N.A. (2007). Slachtoffers en aansprakelijkheid. Een onderzoek naar behoeften, verwachtingen en ervaringen van slachtoffers en hun naasten met betrekking tot het civiele aansprakelijkheidsrecht. Deel I, Terreinverkenning. Den Haag: WODC.

Jaffe, L. L. (1953). Damages for personal injury: the impact of insurance. *Law & Contemporary Problems*. (18), p. 219-39.

Kaplow, L. & Shavell, S. (2002). Economic analysis of law. In A.J. Auerbach & M. Feldstein (eds.), *Handbook of Public Economics*, Volume 3, p. 1661-1784. The Netherlands: Elsevier.

King, J. H. (2004). Pain and suffering, noneconomic damages, and the goals of tort law. *S.M.U.* L. Rev. 18, p. 163-210.

Lindenbergh, S.D. (2008). Smartengeld. 10 jaar later. Rotterdam Institute of Private Law Accepted Paper Series.

MacCoun, R.J. (2005). Voice, Control, and Belonging: The Double-Edged Sword of Procedural Fairness. The Annual Review of Law and Social Science, 1, p. 171-201.

Pryor, E.S. (1993). The Tort Law Debate, Efficiency and the Kingdom of the Ill: A Critique of the Insurance Theory of Compensation. *Virginia Law Review, 91*, p. 91-152.

Relis, T. (2006). Civil litigation from litigants' perspectives: what we know and what we don't know about the litigation experience of individual litigants. *Studies in Law, Politics and Society, 25*, p. 151–212.
Relis, T. (2007). "It's not about the money!": a theory on misconceptions of plaintiffs' litigation aims. *Pittsburgh Law Review*, 68(2), p. 1-48.

Reuters, (2007). *Court considers "Lotto rapist" damages case*. Retrieved on November 12, 2007 from Reuters website: http://www.reuters.com/article/oddlyEnoughNews/idUSN02 55365020071102?feedType=RSS&feedName=oddlyEnoughNews

Schieren, G.A. (1998), The economic framework of personal injury/wrongful death damages. *Journal of Forensic Economics, 11(1)*, p. 33-46.

Schwartz, A. (1988). Proposals for product liability reform: a theoretical syntheses. *The Yale Law Journal, 97(3)*, p. 353-419.

Sen, A. K. (1995). Rationality and Social Choice. *American Economic Review, 85(1)*, p. 1-24.

Sen, A. K. (1997). Maximization and the Act of Choice. *Econometrica, 65(4)*, p. 745-779.

Shapland, J., Willmore, J. & Duff, P. (1985). *Victims in the criminal justice system*. Hants: Gower.

Shavell, S. (2003). *Economic analysis of incident law.* NBER working paper nr. 9482; www.nber.org/papers/w9483. This paper contains the chapters on accident law from Shavell's book: Foundations of Economic analysis of law. Cambridge, Massachusetts: Harvard University Press, 2003.

Shuman, D.W. (1994). The psychology of compensation in court law. *Kansas Law Review, 43*, p. 39-78.

Sunstein, C.R. (2007). *Illusory Losses.* U of Chicago Law & Economics, Olin Working Paper No. 340 Available at SSRN: http://ssrn.com/abstract=983810

Tyler, T.R. (2006). Process utility and help seeking: What do people want from experts? *Journal of Economic Psychology, 27*, p. 360–376.

Verburg, G.J.M. (2009). *Vaststelling van smartengeld.* Deventer: Kluwer.

Viscusi, W.K. (1993). Comments and Discussion on the study of Calfee & Winston: The consumer welfare effects of liability for pain and suffering: an exploratory analysis. *Brookings Papers on Economic Activity. Microeconomics, 1*, p. 175-196.

Viscusi, W.K. (1996). Pain and Suffering: Damages in Search of a Sounder Rationale, *Michigan Law & Policy Review, 1*, p. 141-67.

Viscusi, W.K. (2000). Misuses and proper uses of hedonic values of life. *Journal of Forensic Economics, 13*, p. 111–125.

Viscusi, W.K. (2000a). The value of life in legal context. *American Law and Economics Review, 2(1)*, p. 195-222.

Viscusi, W.K. (2003). *Tort reform and insurance markets.* Harvard Law and Economics Discussion Paper No. 440. Available at SSRN: http://ssrn.com/abstract=469904

Viscusi, W.K. (2008). The value of life. In S. Durlauf and L. Blume (ed.), *New Palgrave Dictionary of Economics and the Law.* London: Macmillan Publishers.

Viscusi, W. Kip, (2008) The Flawed Hedonic Damages Measure for Wrongful Death and Personal Injury Compensation. *Journal of Forensic Economics, Forthcoming.* Available at SSRN: http://ssrn.com/abstract=1084933

Viscusi, W.K. & Evans, W.N. (1990). Utility functions that depend on health status: estimates and economic implications. *American Economic Review, 80*, p. 353-374.

Viscusi, W.K. & Born, P. H. (2005). Damages caps, insurability, and the performance of medical malpractice insurance. *The Journal of Risk and Insurance, 72(1)*, p. 23-43.

"It is usually futile for courts to award heavy damages for personal injuries; the isolated individual offender can rarely make large amends. What, then, could be done to provide the compensation which the victim ought to receive?"

Margery Fry, 1959: p. 192

Financial compensation for victims of crime

Who receives compensation from the Dutch Crime Compensation Fund and how do these victims perceive financial compensation?

By J.D.W.E. Mulder

This chapter is an adaptation of: Mulder, J.D.W.E. (2009). Compensatie na geweld. Wie krijgen er een vergoeding van het Schadefonds Geweldsmisdrijven en wat zijn de effecten van zo'n financiële vergoeding? Tilburg: Intervict/PrismaPrint.

Introduction

In the 1950's, British magistrate Margery Fry published a series of articles in the British newspaper The Observer. In those articles, Fry argued in favour of a state-run compensation programme for victims of violent crime, drawing attention to the inadequacies of civil actions for damages. Fry lamented, for example, a court award of £11.500 to be paid to a man blinded by an assault, where due to the offender's poor financial state, the compensation was ordered to be paid at a rate of 5 shilling per week, a rate which would require 442 years for its recovery (Fry, 1957).

Fry's agitation stirred academic commentary (e.g. Morris, 1961; Schultz, 1965; U. Chi. L. Rev., 1965) and governments to act: New Zealand introduced a crime compensation scheme in 1963, Britain followed in 1964, and California and Wisconsin proceeded in 1965 (O'Connell, 2003). Today, all US states have a state-run crime compensation fund, just like Austria, Australia, Belgium, Bermuda, Canada, Columbia, Denmark, Germany, Finland, France, Hong Kong, Ireland, Israel, Italy, Japan, Luxembourg, the Netherlands, Northern Ireland, Norway, Puerto Rico, Philippines, Poland, Portugal, Scotland, Spain, Sweden, Switzerland, and the United Arab Emirates (O'Connell, 2003).

In short, crime compensation funds can be described as schemes involved in "the granting of public funds to persons who have been victimized by a crime of violence and to persons who survived those killed by such a crime" (Edelhertz & Geis, 1974 as cited by Megret, 2010, p. 6). The reason for granting these funds, according to Miers (2007), is that the public feels a sense of responsibility for, and sympathy with, the innocent victim of a crime of violence. Hence, a financial award from a state fund would represent society's way of acknowledging the harm that has been done to the victim as a representative of the community (Home Office 2005: 14, 21 as cited by Miers, 2007, p. 337).[21]

[21] Theorists have argued that a logical defensible rationale on which to base compensation schemes, like a state's legal liability to victims, or a national insurance rationale, is lacking (see

When the first crime compensation programs were established, scholars lively discussed the possible pros and cons (e.g. Silving, 1959; Schultz, 1965; Mueller, 1965; Cosway, 1973). Soon thereafter, however, scholarly attention for the compensation programs declined. As a consequence, the effects of granting public funds to victims of violent crime have hardly been studied (O'Connell, 2003, p. 20-1). It, for instance, is unknown which victims receive state compensation, how the money affects those victims, and whether they are satisfied with the amounts received.

In order to fill this knowledge gap, a survey was conducted among recipients of the Dutch Crime Compensation Fund. Three theories underlie this survey, namely: procedural justice, therapeutic jurisprudence and the social value of state compensation. To begin with the latter; several authors have purported the social dynamics of state compensation. Duff (1998), for example, argues that a state award represents a broad social statement to the effect that the public sympathizes with the victim in respect of his or her undeserved suffering. State compensation would reflect society's solidarity with the victim (Ligterink & Hermsen, 2006) and society's acknowledgement of the victim's harm (Home Office 2005: 14, 21 as cited by Miers, 2007, p. 337). Yet, whether victims actually perceive a state award as a gesture of society's concern is unknown. Cobley (1998, p. 222) claims that victims of child abuse would indeed view financial compensation as "a public statement of recognition - not only that the abuse took place, but also that someone other than the victim was responsible". Yet, to my knowledge, there is no empirical evidence that confirms her statement, or for that matter, disproves it.

The second theory that underlies the present study, and which is in some way related to that of the social value of state compensation, is that of therapeutic jurisprudence. Therapeutic jurisprudence is recognized as an important model for assessing the impact that various aspects of the legal system has on its participants (Wexler & Wininck, 1996). One views the law as a social force that may produce therapeutic or anti-therapeutic consequences (Feldthusen et al., 2000, p. 67). Maercker & Muller (2004), for instance have shown how social acknowledgement is important to victims; their recovery is connected to positive social reactions which show appreciation for the unique state the victim is in, and which acknowledge the victim's current difficult situation. Other therapeutic factors are: coping with the emotional consequences of crime (Feldthusen et al., 2000, p. 69), the need to see justice done (Orth, 2003), and a reduction of self-blame (Janoff-Bulman, 1985). As a state compensation scheme is part of a nation's legal system, the present study explores its possible therapeutic and anti-therapeutic effects.

Dignan, 2005, p. 44; Duff, 1998, p. 106). One reasons, therefore, that the introduction of state-run compensation schemes owed more to pragmatic considerations. Miers (1978, p. 55) has linked it to the 'politicisation of crime victims', or the need to do something, for example (as cited by Dignan, 2005, p. 44).

The third underlying theory is that of procedural justice. Like the theory of therapeutic jurisprudence, this theory is commonly used in victimologic studies. Procedural justice refers to the idea of fairness in the processes that resolve disputes and allocate resources. In other words, one does not focus on the outcome of a particular procedure, but one studies the fairness of the methods, mechanisms, and processes by which a certain outcome is determined (Lind & Tyler, 1988). With regards to state compensation, it refers to the process by which recipients are granted compensation, instead of the actual amount that victims receive. Reason to make use of this theory is that there is a rich literature that shows that non-monetary matters, like being able to ask questions and to experience polite and respectful treatment, contribute to an individual's well-being, irrespective of the instrumental outcome (Lind & Tyler, 1988; Tyler, 2006: p. 374). Procedural justice has been proven to be of relevance in many different situations (e.g. Stutzer & Frey, 2006; Okimoto & Tyler, 2007; Dolan, Edlin, Tsuchiya & Wailoo, 2007), yet, up till now, it has never been studied whether mere financial matters, like reparation of losses, are affected by procedural justice too.

As noted, the three theories expounded above underlie the survey that was held among recipients of the Dutch Crime Compensation Fund. How this study on victim compensation was set up will be explained in section 1 of this chapter. Subsequently, section 2 offers a general impression of the survey's results and section 3 provides a summery and conclusion.

1. Methodology

1.1. *The Dutch Crime Compensation Fund*

The present study looks into the effects of financial compensations received by victims of violent crime by means of the Dutch Crime Compensation Fund (hereafter: the Fund). This Fund was founded in 1976 by the Dutch Government in order to show solidarity with the innocent victims of severe crimes (Ligterink & Hermsen, 2006). As many nations have established similar funds over the years, the Dutch Crime Compensation Fund is one of the many state-run crime compensation funds that exist around the world (see O'Connell, 2003).

Persons who have become severely injured as a result of a crime of violence are eligible for a financial award from the Dutch Crime Compensation Fund. In other words, victims of crimes like violent theft, rape, domestic violence, and stalking, may file a claim. However, those who have been fully compensated through other means, by the culprit for instance or an insurance provider, are no longer eligible. Moreover, one assumes victims whose financial capacity exceeds 50.000 euro's,[22] to bare the economic costs of the crime themselves.

[22] The Fund defines financial capacity as: "money that is immediately available".

Hence, the Fund operates like a safety net for those who need it the most.[23]

According to recent research, 35.000 victims would annually be eligible for an application with the Fund (Hoogeveen & van Burik, 2008). Yet, the amount of applications was 7059 in 2008, and even less the years before. The coverage rate of the Fund is therefore at most 20%. As a considerable amount of applications is redrawn before the Fund can decide on them, and many applications are not fully completed, the number of applications actually taken into account by the Fund is often considerably lower than the amount of applications received. In 2008, for example, the Fund decided on 5600 applications, of which it granted 4459.

The Fund's application form is intended to gather as much information as possible regarding the crime claimants fell victim to and how it affected them. Victims are not obliged to provide supporting evidence, but those who furnish a copy of a police report, a statement of their physician or the like, do of course have a stronger case.

If the Fund grants one's application, two types of compensation can be awarded. Firstly, *economic compensation* for economic losses like medical expenses and lost income. Secondly, *non-economic compensation*; a financial award for a victim's pain and suffering.[24] The amount of economic compensation that the Fund awards, depends on the costs incurred – up to a maximum of 22.700 euro. Compensation for pain and suffering is determined by use of 8 scales, ranging from 550 to 9.100 euro.[25]

Since 1976, the Fund's upper levels of compensation have only changed twice (see Table 1.1). Persons victimized between 1976 and 1994, were and still are, eligible for an amount of economic compensation up to 11.350 euro, and for an amount of non-economic compensation ranging between 227 and 4550 euro. In 1994 compensation levels almost doubled: victims could from then on receive up to 22.700 for their economic losses, and between 454 and 9.076 for their pain and suffering. In July 2002, non-economic compensation levels were set at the present amounts of 550 and 9.100 euro.

As the Fund is not allowed to correct for inflation, one could argue that the upper limits have decreased significantly over time: if we assume an annual depreciation rate of 2%, the maximum amount of compensation that could

[23] Victims are not obliged to try other paths to compensation before they file a claim with the Fund. One does not even have to report the crime to the police, or to hold the offender accountable for that matter.

[24] According to Dutch law, close relatives and surviving next of kin are not entitled to claim damages for their pain and suffering. Hence, non-economic compensation is only awarded by the Fund to direct victims.

[25] A standardized list of physical injuries plus an evaluation of the nature, circumstances, and consequences of the crime determines the level of non-economic compensation that the Fund awards.

be granted to a victim of violent crime has dropped by 37% since 1994.

Table 1.1: Dutch Crime Compensation Fund may award up to 31.800 euro

Time frame	Economic compensation limits	Non-economic compensation limits
1976-1994	0-11.350 euro	227-4550 euro
1994-2002	0-22.700 euro	454-9.076 euro
2002-present	0-22.700 euro	550-9.100 euro

1.2. *The respondents*

In February and March 2009, 1000 victims, who had received compensation from the Dutch Crime Compensation Fund in 2008, were approached for participation. All were sent a letter that explained the purpose of the study and invited them to fill out an online questionnaire (see appendix 1). For those who did not have access to the World Wide Web or preferred to complete the measures by pencil, a paper version of the questionnaire was enclosed with the letter.

Out of 225 returned copies, 217 were useable for analysis. This group of 217 is called the net sample of the study. In addition to the questionnaire, it was possible to retrieve information from the files kept by the Crime Compensation Fund. These files provided not only additional information about the 1000 victims approached, but as well about the 100 victims who initially tested the questionnaire. Hence, the study does not only contain a net sample of 217, but also a gross sample of 1100 recipients of state compensation. In the remainder of the report, it is explicitly mentioned when the gross sample is used instead of the net sample.

Whilst the net sample cannot be taken as representative of all the Fund's recipients as a whole, there is no reason to believe that it is atypical. A comparison of the net sample with the gross sample, for example, shows resemblance between the two on aspects like gender, age and type of crime (see table 1.2).

Table 1.2: Comparison of net sample (N=217) with gross sample (N=1100)

	Females	Males	Age	Severe crime	Less severe crime	Total award
Net sample	52%	48%	38 (SD=19)	35%	65%	3120 euro
Gross sample	52%	48%	36 (SD=16)	33%	67%	3160 euro

Finally, I would like to stress that all respondents discussed in this paper are victims who did receive financial reparation from the Dutch Crime Compensation Fund. So, in other words, this report is not about victims applying for financial reparation, or about victims of violent crime in general; it reflects the situation and opinions of actual recipients of state compensation.

1.3. *The survey*

The survey that was held among recipients of the Dutch Crime Compensation Fund was based on three theories, namely procedural justice, therapeutic jurisprudence and the social value of state compensation, as explained in the introduction. Which particular topics were covered by the questionnaire and what kind of content was retrieved from the Fund's files, will be explained concisely, below.

1. First of all, information was collected about the crime and the culprit.
- Type of crime: in order to distinguish between victims, information from the Fund's files was retrieved about the type of crime that recipients were victimized by. After all, victimization by crime is not a homogeneous experience. Victims of rape, for instance, see themselves confronted with a different situation than do victims of violent robbery.
- Knowledge about the culprit: Since the Dutch Crime Compensation Fund operates like a safety-net for those not able to recoup compensation elsewhere, recipients were asked whether they knew who the culprit was and whether they had tried to hold him accountable for their losses.

2. Secondly, information was gathered about the following personal characteristics of recipients:
- Age
- Nationality
- Income
- Gender

3. Thirdly, various aspects of the Fund's procedure were studied. The literature on procedural justice shows that victims' needs relating to the procedure can be distinguished into three factors: 1) respectful and fair treatment, 2) information concerning the process and outcome of their cases, and 3) possibilities for participation (Strang, 2002). Since these factors relate to multiple stages of the Fund's application process, the following division was made:

Before the application
- Knowledge about one's eligibility: research shows that information about the possibilities in the criminal justice system is important to victims (Sims & Myhill, 2001). However, often that information is not sufficiently available (Groenhuijsen & Pemberton, 2009). Seeing the Fund's low

coverage-rate, it seems valuable to know how victims learned about the Fund, which was asked in the survey.

The application itself

- Time between crime and application: according to Young (2003), victims would prefer to receive compensation as soon as possible. Consequently, one might expect victims to apply with a state compensation fund shortly after their victimization. On the other hand, it might take victims a while to cope (see Foa & Rothbaum, 1998) and to find the strength to enter the application process. Moreover, victims might prefer to await the conclusion of a criminal trial against the offender. Hence, it seems interesting to know how much time actually passes between the time of victimization and one's application with a state fund. In order to answer this question, information was retrieved from the Fund's files.
- Motives to file an application: in order to study whether victims apply out of mere financial reasons, or with therapeutic expectations, like acknowledgement and justice being done (Feldthusen et al., 2000), respondents to the survey were asked to elaborate on their motives for filling a claim with the Fund.
- Participation: do recipients file the application with the fund themselves? And if so, how did that affect them? From a procedural justice perspective, it is beneficial to victims to participate in their case (Tyler, 1990). However, increased participation could also lead to psychological stress, especially for those who have developed traumatic disorder as a consequence of the event (Pemberton, 2010, p. 79; Cheon & Regehr, 2006). To so how the application process affects victims, the survey contained several questions concerning that process.

The Fund's decision

- Respect & information: as noted, victims value information and a respectful and fair treatment. So how do recipients experience the time they have to wait for the fund to make its decision? Do recipients think the fund operates in a timely manner? And did the fund kept them properly informed about the progress of their case? Moreover, do victims believe the fund's process is a fair one? And does the fund treat them with sufficient respect?

4. Fourthly, recipients were questioned about the outcome of the procedure: the financial compensation granted by the Fund.

- Amount of compensation received: how much economic and non-economic compensation do recipients receive?
- Satisfaction: are recipients satisfied with the amount of financial reparation they receive? One might expect that the more one receives, the more satisfied one is. Is that the case here too?
- Expectations: does the amount of money awarded by the fund match the recipients' expectations? Or do victims expect to receive more form the fund?

5. Finally, information was collected about the social value and therapeutic effects of receiving financial compensation from a state-run compensation fund.

- Social value: as explained earlier, the money awarded by state funds is said to represent a broad social statement, which reflects the public's sympathy with the victim in respect of his or her undeserved suffering (Duff, 1995). Do recipients of the Ditch Fund perceive the compensation they receive in a similar way?
- Therapeutic effects: does the Dutch Crime Compensation Fund produce therapeutic consequences (Winkler & Wexler, 1996)? Does it, for instance, offer social acknowledgement (Maercker & Muller, 2004)? Or does it help victims to cope with the emotional consequences of their victimization, do they see justice done (Orth, 2003), and does it reduce victims' self-blame (Janoff-Bulman, 1985)?

The survey's results will be described in the upcoming paragraph.

2. Results

2.1. Characteristics of recipients and their victimization

As noted, the Dutch Crime Compensation Fund awards financial compensation to thousands of victims, yearly. This paragraph discusses the peculiar characteristics of these recipients and the crimes that have been committed against them. Subsequently these characteristics are compared to information available about Dutch crimes and victims in general.

2.1.1. Type of crime

Those who receive a financial award from the Dutch Crime Compensation Fund, all fell victim to a violent crime. Crimes recognized by the Fund can be categorized as follows:[26]

- Homicide and manslaughter
- Attempted homicide and manslaughter
- Severe sexual crimes (amongst others: (mandatory)rape, involuntarily prostitution, intercourse with someone under the age of 12)
- Sexual crimes (among others: fornication, (attempted) sexual violation)
- Violent theft
- Assault and battery
- Severe assaults (among others: hostage taking, kidnapping and severe physical abuse)
- Threats (among others: extortion and stalking)

[26] Categorization of crimes has been done in accordance with the Fund.

If we categorize recipients by the above mentioned categories, it becomes apparent that one in twelve recipients suffered (attempted) homicide or manslaughter, and one in eight suffered a severe sexual crime, like rape. As table 2.1 shows, the most prevalent crimes among recipients are violent theft and common assaults (respectively 24% and 29% of cases).

Table 2.1: Types of crime suffered by successful applicants of the Fund (N=1100)

Type of crime	Percentage of applicants
Homicide and manslaughter	2
Attempted homicide and manslaughter	6
Severe sexual crimes	13
Sexual crimes	7
Violent theft	24
Assault and battery	29
Severe assault	11
Threat	7
Total	100

Table 2.1 shows as well how the majority (about two thirds) of recipients of the Dutch Crime Compensation Fund awards fell victim to one of the relatively less severe crimes; threats, common assaults, violent theft and minor sexual offences. The remainder suffered the more severe offences: (attempted) homicide or manslaughter, severe assault and severe sexual violence.

Table 2.2: Reported violent crime in the Netherlands in 2007[27]

Types of violent crime	Percentage of reports
(Attempted) Homicide and manslaughter	1
Rape	1
Indecent assault	2
Other forms of sexual violence	2
Violent theft	12
Assault	54
Threat	27
Extortion	1
Total	100

[27] See Kalidien & Eggen (2009). 'Criminaliteit en Rechtshandhaving 2008. Ontwikkelingen en samenhangen' the Hague: Boom Juridische Uitgevers.

The Fund's statistics show divergence from the general police figures. Table 2.2 contains reported violent crime in the Netherlands in 2007.[28] Although the categories differ slightly from those used by the Fund, it is apparent that more severe crimes are overrepresented in the population of applicants to the Fund.

2.1.2. *Recipients' age*

The age range of victims who receive an award from the Dutch Crime Compensation Fund is wide. Some recipients have not even celebrated their first birthday, while others are over eighty years old. Most recipients (29%), however, are between fifteen and twenty-five years of age, see Figure 2.1. The overrepresentation of young people is not surprising, as they also run the highest risk of falling victim to violence.[29]

Figure 2.1: Recipients' age (N=1100)

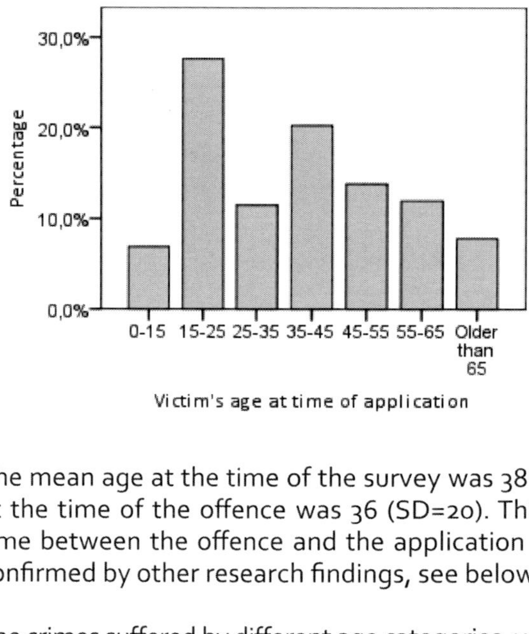

The mean age at the time of the survey was 38 (SD=19) while the mean age at the time of the offence was 36 (SD=20). This suggests that the average time between the offence and the application is about two years, which is confirmed by other research findings, see below.

The crimes suffered by different age categories, vary considerably. A majority of the youngest age category (under fifteen years), for instance, suffered a sexual offence, while hardly anyone over 55 suffered such a crime. Recipients older than 45, on their turn, are overrepresented among cases of violent theft. Most young adults (15 through 35 years of age) suffered an assault (see table 2.3).

---

28 At the time of writing the report, these were the most recent figures available.

29 See also Wittebrood, K. (2006) 'Slachtoffers van criminaliteit' The Hague, Sociaal Cultureel Planbureau (p. 69).

Table 2.3: Overview of types of crime per age category (N=1100)

Type of crime	Percentage of cases per age category							
	0-15	15-25	25-35	35-45	45-55	55-65	>65	Total
Homicide and manslaughter	1	1	4	3	2	4	2	2
Attempted homicide and manslaughter	7	6	6	5	7	8	7	6
Severe sexual offences	31	20	10	10	4	9	2	13
Sexual offences	27	10	6	2	2	-	0	7
Violent theft	4	15	18	28	39	45	45	24
Assault & battery	17	31	36	29	26	23	31	29
Severe assaults	6	12	10	13	13	7	9	11
Threat	7	5	10	10	8	4	2	7
Total	100%	100%	100%	100%	100%	100%	100%	100%

2.1.3. *Recipient's Gender*

In general crime statistics, men are overrepresented as offenders *and* as victims (Wittebrood, 2006, p. 69).[30] Yet, among respondents, the majority, 52%, is female (N=1100).[31] The crime suffered is by recipients is clearly related to gender, as table 2.4 shows. In line with general victimological findings, women suffer a large majority of all sexual offences, while men more often fall victim to (common) assaults (Wittebrood, 2006, p. 68-9).

Table 2.4: Type of crime by gender (N=1100)

Type of crime	Males	Females
Homicide and manslaughter	2	3
Attempted homicide and manslaughter	10	3
Severe sexual crimes	2	24
Sexual crimes	2	10
Violent theft	25	24
Assault & battery	36	23
Severe assaults	18	5
Threats	5	10
Total	100%	100%

30 See also Van Dijk, J.J.M., Manchin, R., van Kesteren, J.N. & Hideg, G. (2007).

31 The survey results do not provide an explanation for this finding. It is for instance unclear whether more man than women apply with the Fund, and that women's applications have a higher chance of being granted, or that simply more females seek help in the aftermath of violent crime.

A noteworthy finding is that 60% of the recipients who suffered a completed homicide and manslaughter is female, against only 23% of the recipients of *attempted* homicide and manslaughter. This is probably a reflection of the fact that significantly more men than women die as a result of homicide and manslaughter. In 2008, for example, 125 men were killed versus 50 women.[32] In other words, more women than men become surviving next of kin (which explains the majority of females among recipients in case of homicide and manslaughter), and less women than men become the victim of an attempted homicide or manslaughter (which explains the low percentage of women amongst recipients of an award for attempted homicide and manslaughter).

2.1.4. *Recipients' nationality*

A substantial proportion of the Dutch population has a non-Dutch ethnic background. On January 2008, 20% of the population was estimated to be '*allochthonous*'.[33] Nevertheless only 8% of the participants in the surveyhas a foreign nationality, mostly Moroccan, Turkish or Surinam.

There are three possible explanations for this discrepancy. The first would be that ethnic minorities stand a smaller chance of falling victim to crime. This, however, is not likely to be true. Although there is some disagreement concerning this subject, most research shows minorities run a larger rather than a smaller risk of victimization. [34]

The second and third possible reasons seem more likely to explain the relatively low participation rate of ethnic minorities. First of all, in survey research in general (Feskens, 2009), and in victimization surveys in the Netherlands in particular (van Mierlo & Pemberton, 2009), ethnic minorities are less likely to participate, at least unless far more extensive attempts to reach them are used. Secondly, eligible victims from ethnic minorities might be less likely to access the Dutch Crime Compensation Fund. More research is needed into this subject, but there are indications that the latter might be may be true.[35]

---

32 Central Bureau of Statistics, 2009: victims of homicide and manslaughter in 2008.

33 Central Bureau of Statistics: www.cbs.nl: information about the population, gender, age and descent.

34 See Van Dijk et al, 2007.

35 A noteworthy observation is that ethnic minorities are underrepresented among the clientele of Victim Support the Netherlands (Hanrath, 2002). This could not only signal smaller coverage of victims from ethnic minorities by victim focused organisations in general, but Victim Support is also one of the largest referring organisations to the Fund. Relatively poor access of ethnic minorities to Victim Support can then have a direct negative impact on their access to the Fund.

2.1.5. *Recipients' income*

As noted, the Dutch Crime Compensation Fund is supposed to act as a safety net. Only costs that cannot be recouped through any other channel, - the offender, an insurance provider, etc.- are eligible for the Fund's awards. Moreover, one assumes victims who have a financial capital of more than 50.000 euro to bare the economic cost of crime themselves.

This brings us to the question whether there are income differences among recipients. Is the Dutch Fund a safety net especially for lower social-economic classes? Or do victims of all social classes receive state compensation?

According to the survey results, the latter is true: recipients' from all social classes receive state compensation (see Table 2.5). However, recipients from the lower social-economic classes are clearly overrepresented. As Table 2.5 reveals, 36% of recipients have a disposable annual income of less than 10.000 euro, while this applies to only 5% of the Dutch population.[36] Conversely, 26% of the Dutch population has an annual disposable income of over 40.000 euro, while only 3% of the recipients of the Fund's awards has that much to spend.

It therefore appears that the Fund acts mainly as a safety net for victims from lower social-economic classes, although one should bear in mind that the lower social economic classes are also overrepresented in victimization statistics (Kalidien & Eggen, 2009, p. 59).

Table 2.5: Recipients from lower socio-economic classes are overrepresented (N=217)

Annual disposable income	Recipients	Dutch population in general
Less than 10.000 euro	36	5
Between 10 and 20.000 euro	29	25
Between 20 and 30.000 euro	12	25
Between 30 and 40.000 euro	6	19
More than 40.000 euro	3	26
Do not know	15	0
Total	100%	100%

2.1.6. *Do recipients know the offender?*

It is common knowledge that many crimes are never resolved. In the Netherlands, the clear-up rate for reported violent crime (as reported in table 2.2) is approximately 60% (Central Bureau of Statistics, 2008). Yet, the survey

36 The disposable income was defined by the recipient's total personal income minus personal current taxes.

results reveal that when asked about the culprit of their victimization, 76% of the recipients indicate to know who the offender was (N=217). Compared to the general clear-up rate, this percentage is rather high.[37]

The survey results also show that more than half (52%) of the recipients who knew the culprit, have tried to recoup damages from him. This attempt, however, failed in the majority of cases. Less than 1 out of 5 (18%) actually received payment from the offender and a many of these victims failed to secure full compensation.

Recipients, who knew the culprit but refrained from recouping damages, had various reasons to do so. The respondents in the survey mentioned the following motives (N=70):

- The offender is a family member/acquaintance (20%),
- I could not cope with the emotional stress (20%)
- The offender did not have the means to compensate me (19%)
- Problems with the criminal justice procedure (in 16% there either had not been a court case against the offender, was the victim not informed about the handling of the case, or the final verdict had not been reached yet).

2.1.7. *Summary*

The characteristics of the recipients of an award from the Fund deviate from both victims of violent crime and the Dutch population as a whole. Recipients generally fall into the lower income categories. Ethnic minorities are underrepresented in this study. This could either be due to their higher non-response rate in victimological surveys, or could signal that ethnic minorities face additional barriers in accessing the Fund. Victims of severe violent crime and female victims of crime are overrepresented in comparison with general victimization statistics.

Various characteristics are interrelated. Male recipients receive awards for different types of crime than female recipients and the same is true for victims from different age categories. Only 8% of the recipients in this survey received (partial) compensation from the offender. The offender is known to most of the respondents. Over half attempts to recoup their damages from the offender, but this fails in most cases.

2.2. *The procedure*

This paragraph discusses the recipients experiences with the Fund's procedures to determine eligibility for compensation and the amount of compensation. It addresses the folowing time frames:

---

37 Idem.

- Before the application
- The application itself
- Waiting for the Fund's decision
- Looking back on the decision

2.3. *Before applying*

2.3.1. *How did victims learn about the possibility to apply?*

Research shows that information about the possibilities in the criminal justice system is important to victims (Sims & Myhill, 2001). However, often that information is not sufficiently available (Groenhuijsen & Pemberton, 2009). Seeing the low coverage-rate of the fund (20%), respondents to the survey were asked how they discovered they were eligible to apply for state compensation. The answers provided to this question show that the majority of recipients (60%) were referred to the Fund by Victim Support the Netherlands. 17% was told by the police, 14% by a lawyer and 7% was told by family or friends (see table 2.6).

Tabel 2.6: Most recipients learn about state compensation through Victim Support

Referrers	Percentage of recipients referred
Victim Support the Netherlands	60
The police	17
A lawyer	14
Family/friends	7
Newspapers/magazins/internet	5
Other (emplyer/counseler)	7
Don't know	3
Total	113

* Due to the fact that respondents could choose more than one referral option, total adds up to more than 100%

2.3.2. *Time passed since the offence*

According to Cobley (1998, p. 232) it would be best if victims received compensation as soon as possible after the crime. Moreover, Young (2003, p. 10) states that that most victims would prefer compensation as quickly as possible. Since the Dutch Crime Compensation Fund offers victims the chance to apply for an award in the immediate aftermath of their victimization, one would expect victims to claim compensation shortly after the crime. The survey results, however, reveal that there exists an average period of more than 1,5 years (20 months) between the victimization and application with the Fund (N=1100).

The time passed between the offence and application with the Fund shows large variation (SD=43 months). Some recipients apply within in a week, while others wait more than 30 years; table 2.7 provides an overview. Just under half (46%) of the applications occurs within 6 months, while a little over a quarter occurs within three months. In 34% it takes more than a year to apply, while in 4% of cases more than 10 years have passed since the offence.

Table 2.7: While 89% of police reports are filled within one month after the crime, only 12% of recipients apply for compensation within one month after the crime (N=1100)

Time passed	Percentage of applications to the Fund	Percentage of reports to the police
Less than 1 month	12	89
1 through 3 months	16	2
3 though 6 months	18	2
6 through 12 months	20	2
1 through 5 years	27	3
5 through 10 years	3	2
More than 10 years	4	1
Total	100%	101%

Table 2.7 also shows the period between the occurence of the offence and the report of the crime to the police; 89% reports the crime within a month. The time lag for application is therefore not due to the time between the offence and the police report. What does explain the considerable amount of time between the victimization and an application with the fund is unclear. Possibly, victims prefer the criminal case to have run its course before going to the Crime Compensation Fund or is it that victims have to go through a long and arduous coping process before they apply for compensation.

Table 2.8: Victims of sexual crimes wait the longest before applying for compensation (N=1100)

Type of crime	Average time between crime and application in months (sd)
Homicide and manslaughter	33 (56)
Attempted homicide and manslaughter	16 (22)
Severe sexual crimes	46 (67)
Sexual crimes	69 (96)
Violent theft	7 (13)
Assault & battery	13 (21)
Severe assault	12(20)
Threat	15 (23)
Total	20 (43)

Table 2.8. shows there is considerable variation in the average time passed between the crime and the application at the Fund depending on the type of crime suffered by the victim. Victims of theft, for instance 'only' wait seven months (SD=13 months), while victims of sexual crimes wait generally almost more than 6 years (SD= 96 months). Accoring to the Krukal-Wallis test there is a significant difference between the various types of crime ($H(7)=187$, $p=.000$). What causes this dfferences, however, is here too, not immediately apparent.

2.3.3. *The application itself*

2.3.3.1. Reasons for submitting an application

The Dutch Crime Compensation Fund awards financial compensation to victims of violent crime. As this is the only service the Fund offers, it may seem apparent that victims' main or even sole reason for applying is financial. Yet, according to Feldthusen et al. (2000, p. 75) victims enter such a process with explicit therapeutic expectations; they see the claiming process as having a role in the recovery of their well being. This raises the question why Dutch victims apply with a crime compensation fund? Do they apply out of therapeutic or financial motives? Or perhaps both?

During the survey respondents were asked to explain in their own words why they had submitted a claim with the Fund. Answers given to this question differed considerably, some used a few words, other used half a page. Nevertheless, three general motives for application could be distinguished. First of all, most recipients describe a financial motive (44%). Respondents indicate for example, that compensation was sought to cover legal costs, moving expenses, or as a matter of principle. Secondly, one in four victims

(26%), mention therapeutic expectations.[38] Receiving acknowledgement as a victim, and finding closure are important reasons for victims to apply. Thirdly, almost 10% says to have submitted a claim because they were (strongly) advized to do so by either Victim Support, their lawyer or the police.

The remaining respondents either did not remember why they filed a claim (15%) or mentioned other motives (6%).

2.3.3.2. Filing an application

Victims who believe to be eligible for compensation can file an application for an award. To this end they have to fill out and submit an application form. Potential recipients can request a form from the Fund or obtain the form from the Fund's website.

The survey reveals that many recipients do not fill out the form themselves. Almost one in two (47%) allows someone else to fill out the form (for instance a Victim Support-worker or a lawyer). Those recipients who did fill out the form themselves, needed approximately 4,5 hours to do so. For a majority of them, this was a stressful experience. Measured on a 1 thru 10 stress-scale, 60% of the respondents reported a level of 6 or higher. The data shows that the stress level is directly correlated with the time necessary for filling out the form: the longer this takes, the more stress the recipient experiences (r_s=.380, two sided, N=88).

Nevertheless most respondents do not think the application form contains unnecessary questions. Two thirds indicate the application form does not pose any unnecessary questions, while only 2% thinks it contains many unnecessary questions.

Since hardly any respondent complained about the amount or type of questions posed on the Fund's application form, while many mentioned the difficulty of being reminded of the crime in such detail, is seems likely that the stress that respondents experience while filling out the application form, is due to the unhappy memories that the form triggers. Many victims of crime experience stress when they have to recall facts surrounding their victimization (see Foa & Rothbaum, 1998), so filling out the form may be experienced as a prolonged confrontation with the memories of victimization and therefore elicit stressful feelings on the part of the victim.

2.3.3.3. Knowledge about the Fund's way of working

Once victims have send in their application form, they have to wait for the Fund's decion. Do recipients know how the fund decides on the applications

38 A majority mentioned therapeutic expectations exclusively.

it receives? The survey results show that almost one in two recipients does not. The following quote from a respondent illustrates this clearly: 'I think the Fund's decision process is very strange. You receive a sum of money, but no explanation of how this has been calculated. My brother and I suffered the same crime, but received different awards'.

2.3.3.4. Waiting for the decision

On average it takes the Dutch Crime Compensation Fund 2.5 months to reach a decision. Some victims will be notified within a month, while others may have to be patient for nearly a year (SD=2 months; N=1100) (see table 2.9).

Most victims are positive about the time lag between application and decision. Only 19% thought it took too long, while 41% thought it went rather quick (see table 2.10). Those who had to wait a long period of time are precisely those who call the Fund's processing slow (rjonkheere-terpstra= 0,378). Moreover, the recipients who had to wait a long period of time, are also those who experience stress due to the long wait (rs=0,141, N=214, p< 0,01). The recipients who found the process to be completed swiftly do not experience additional stress.

Table 2.9: Number of months it takes the Fund to proces recipients' application forms (N=1100)

Number of months	Percentage of cases
0	8
1	24
2	33
3	12
4	12
5	5
6	1
7	2
› 7	3
Total	100%

Table 2.10 : Recipients' opinion about the processing of their case (N=217)

Opinion	Percentage of cases
Very slow	5
Slow	14
Neither quick/nor slow	40
Quick	34
Very quick	7
Total	100%

2.3.4. *Looking back on the decision*

The survey reveals that recipients are reasonably satisfied about the Fund's information concerning the progress of the application. 60% of respondents said sufficient information was provided, while 22% was not satisfied with the manner in which the Fund kept them abreast of the progress of their cases (see tabel 2.11).

Tabel 2.11: Do recipients think they are well enough informed about the progress of their case? (N=217)

Opinion	Percentage of cases
Not well informed	7
Not really well informed	15
Indifferent	12
Rather wel informed	10
Well informed	50
Don't know	7
Total	101%

A large majority of the respondents has no qualms with the fairness of the application of the process. Over three quarters of recipients is of the opinion that the process is fair, while only 12% finds it to be more or less unfairble (see table 2.12).

Table 2.12: How fair do recipients think the Fund handled their case? (N=217)

Opinion	Percentage of cases
Highly unfair	2
Unfair	3
Not unfair or fair	7
Fair	54
Highly fair	24
Don't know	11
Total	101%

In a similar vein a majority (60%) is convinced that the Fund sufficiently reviewed the specific circumstances of their case. One in six of the respondents thought the Fund did not do this sufficiently (see table 2.13).

Table 2.13: Did the Fund suffieciently review the specific circumstances of the case according to recipients? (N=217)

Opinion	Percentage of cases
Not at all	5
Very little	11
Neutral	12
Somewhat	7
To a great extent	54
Don't know	12
Total	101%

Finally, according to a majority of recipients the Fund treats them with sufficient respect. Over 80% of victims states that the Fund always treated them with adequate respect and recognition. In fact only 1% was not entirely satisfied with the level of respectful treatment (see Table 2.14).

Table 2.14: Has the Crime Compensation Fund treated recipeint in a respectful manner? (N=217)

Opinion	Percentage of cases
Most definitely not	-
Definitely not	-
Not really	1
Neutral	12
Slightly	2
Certainly	42
Most certainly	40
Don't know	4
Total	101%

2.3.5. *Summary*

In general recipients are positive about the Fund's application process. From a procedural justice perspecitve it is clear that recipients believe the Fund's treatment is fair and respectful. Moreover, most victims are positive about the time lag between their application and the Fund's decision and the way the Fund informs them about its progres. However, recipients have fairly little knowledge about the way the Fund reaches it decisions, and a majority is referred to the Fund by Victim Support Netherlands. These results reveal shortcomings in the information provided to applicants.

Many victims experience elevated stress levels when filling out a form. As it is likely that the memories of victimization are the cause of these elevations, this might not be completely avoided. Nevertheless, awareness of the stress caused by the application process and vigilance concerning possible avenues to reduce the stress, is advisable.

Finally, it is noteworthy that almost one in three recipients filed a claim with the fund out of therapeutic reasons. Receiving acknowledgement, for instance, was an objective commonly expressed by respondents.

2.4. *Financial awards*

If the Dutch Crime Compensation Fund considers a victim's application to be eligible, the corresponding compensation award is paid out to the victim within a matter of weeks. This chapter discusses the awards granted to recipients, and whether the grants met victims' expectations and delivered them satisfaction. Analysis were done seperatly for the total award, compensation for economic damages and that for non-economic damages.

2.5. *Total award*[39]

The average award granted by the Fund in 2008 was 3.160 euro (N=1100). The variation is considerable; totals awards vary from a few hundred euro to a maximum payment of 28.000 euro (SD= 3065 euro). Table 2.15 provides a breakdown of awards into 9 categories. The modal category is that of 2500-5000 euro.

Table 2.15: Classes of total awards in 2008 (N=1100)

Total award	Percentage of cases
0-500 euro	2
500-1000 euro	19
1000-1500 euro	11
1500-2000 euro	7
2000-2500 euro	7
2500-5000 euro	42
5000-10000 euro	9
10000-25000 euro	3
Over 25.000 euro	0,5
Total	100,5%

Based on the fact that the Fund could award victims up to 31.800 euro, one could argue the Fund's grants are rather modest. Nevertheless, 36% of the respondents indicated they received more compensation than initially expected. 27% received less than expected and in only 13% of cases the award matched the recipient's expectations (see table 2.16)

Table 2.16: Did the award meet the recipients expectations? (N=217)

The award was...	Percentage of cases
Much lower than the recipient had expected	12
Slightly lower than the recipient had expected	15
What the recipient had expected	13
Slightly higher than the recipient had expected	16
Much higher than the recipient had expected	20
Do not know	24
Total	100%

39 Due to differences in methods of calculation these figures differ slightly from those the Fund mentions in her own annual report.

Although the granted awards are often not in line with victims' expectations, most recipients are satisfied with the award. 75% is at least moderately satisfied, while only 17% is unsatisfied, see table 2.17.

Table 2.17: Satisfaction with total award (N=217)

Satisfaction with total award	Percentage of cases
Very unsatisfied	6
Satisfied	7
Moderately satisfied	4
Not satisfied or unsatisfied	6
Moderately satisfied	13
Satisfied	35
Very satisfied	27
Do not know	2
Total	100%

There is a clear correlation between expectations and satisfaction: of the victims who received more than expected, 97% was (very) satisfied. Of the victims who received what they thought they would, 89% was (very) satisfied, of those who received less only 48% was satisfied (Chi square=47,726: df= 2, N=153, p<0,001; Somer's D=0,359).

Noteworthy is that there is no correlation between the amount of money that victims received and their level of satisfaction (Kruskal-Wallis, H(6)=11.197, ns). So receiving more money does not automatically translate into higher levels of satisfaction.

2.5.1. *Economic compensation*

Every victim of violent crime may apply for an award from the Dutch Crime Compensation Fund. The compensation for economic damages is, however, restricted to bodily harm; only costs relating to physical damages, which are a direct consequence of the crime, are eligible. In addition the Fund requires evidence of the costs made, in the shape of receipts and the like.

Table 2.18: Amounts of economic compensation granted (gross sample: N=1100)

Economic compensation	Percentage of cases
No economic compensation awarded	23
1-500 euro	46
500-1000 euro	12
1000-1500 euro	5
1500-2000 euro	3
2000-2500 euro	2
2500-5000 euro	5
5000-10000 euro	2
10000-22.700 euro	2
Total	101%

The maximum amount the Fund can award for economic damages is 22.700 euro. Yet, this amount is hardly ever granted. Indeed, as Table 2.18 shows, even awards exceeding 5.000 euro are a seldom occurrence (N=1100). This is most likely due to the high levels of insurance coverage in the Netherlands;[40] most victims will be covered for economic damages like medical expenses and lost income.

The mean award granted to recipients for economic damages was 980 euro in 2008. However, almost half (48%) of the recipients received less than 100 euro. Moreover, in 23% of cases no award was granted for economic damages at all. Hence, the lion's share of the awards the Fund grants, is in order to compensate non-economic damages, i.e. pain and suffering.

2.5.2. *Compensation for pain and suffering*

Every direct victim is entitled to receive compensation for the pain and suffering they experienced due to their victimisation. The indirect victims of homicide (i.e. relatives/ dependents of victims of homicide) are normally not eligible for this type of compensation, although there are exceptions to this rule.[41]

Unlike the award for economic damages the victim is not required to provide

40 Although the Netherlands has only 16,5 million inhabitants, the Dutch insurance market accounts for 2,5% of the insurance premiums paid worldwide. In 2009 life and nonlife insurance premiums (excluding cross-border business) amounted to 13.6 percent of Dutch gross domestic product (GDP) (International Insurance Fact Book 2010). As insurance is not particularly expensive in the Netherlands, one reasons the Dutch are largely risk-averse and spend yearly 4600 euro each on different insurance policies (CEA Statistics, 2009).

41 See www.schadefonds.nl

evidence of the costs of pain and suffering, yet may be required to provide evidence of the occurrence of pain and suffering.[42] The Fund's awards for pain and suffering are determined by use of 8 scales; depending on the crime and its consequences, the Fund can award 550 tot 9.100 euro.[43] For example, a victim of a robbery who suffers minor flesh wounds receives 1400 euro (second scale), while a victim of aggravated rape with severe bodily damage receive € 8.250 (seventh scale).

As is apparent from table 2.19, most victims fall in the two lowest scales (47%). In addition, the fourth scale contains 25% of recipients. The mean award for non-economic damages is 2185 euro (SD 1533 euro). Hence, on average, two thirds of the total award that victims receive is related to non-economic damages (N=1100).

Table 2.19: Awards for non-economic damages (N=1100)

Scale and award	Percentage of cases
I € 550	26
II € 1.400	21
III € 2.100	10
IV € 2.750	25
V € 4.150	15
VI € 5.500	2
VII € 8.250	0,3
VIII € 9.100	0,2
Total	99,5%

The awards for similar crimes vary considerably. Some victims of severe sexual violence, for instance, receive 550 euro, while others may receive over 8000 euro, see table 2.20. This is probably due to differences in the consequences of similar crimes.

42 In case of certain crimes, like sexual offences, the Fund automatically assumes pain and suffering, and the victim has then nothing to prove.

43 See www.schadefonds.nl for an overview of categories and awards.

Table 2.20: Awards for non-economic damages by type of crime (N=1100)

Scales	Homicide & man-slaughter	Attemped H&M	Severe sexual crimes	Sexual crimes	Violent theft	Assault & battery	Severe assaults	Threat
I € 550		13%	1%	30%	21%	43%	30%	25%
II € 1.400		29%	4%	26%	8%	28%	25%	32%
III € 2.100		10%	1%	4%	4%	18%	16%	9%
IV € 2.750		15%	33%	24%	50%	6%	17%	28%
V € 4.150	100%	22%	47%	16%	16%	4%	10%	6%
VI € 5.500		7%	13%			2%	2%	
VII € 8.250		1,5%	1%		,4%		1%	
VIII € 9.100		1,5%			,4%		1%	
Total	100%	100%	100%	100%	100%	100%	100%	100%

The survey reveals that recipients are satisfied with the award for non-economic damages, like they were concerning the total award. 76% is at least somewhat satisfied, while only a minority of 14% is dissatisfied. Again, it is noteworthy that the satisfaction experienced is unrelated to the amount received (Chi-square = 3.878, df=2, N=132, ns).

Table 2.21: Satisfaction with compensation for non-economic damages (N=156)

Satisfaction with non-economic compensation	Percentage of cases
Very dissatisfied	5
Dissatisfied	3
Slighty dissatisfied	6
Not satisfied or unsatisfied	10
Slightly satisfied	15
Satisfied	39
Very satisfied	18
Do not know	5
Total	100%

2.6. *Summary*

The results clearly reveal that recipients are satisfied with the awards granted by the Fund. On average an award amounts to 3160 euro. The lion's share of this award (about 2/3), is granted for non-economic damages. Many victims do not receive any compensation for economic damages.

The awards often do not meet victims' expectations: in both a negative and a positive sense. Only 13% of victims received the award they had expected while others received more or less than anticipated. Victims' satisfaction with the award closely resembles the extent to which the award meets or exceeds their expectations, rather than the absolute level of the award granted. Matching expectations with outcomes therefore seems a more important element of preventing dissatisfaction, then simply raising the amount awarded.

2.7. *Therapeutic effects and social value*

To gain insight into the consequences of receiving state compensation, respondents were queried about their (emotional) responses to the receipt of an award. Many of the emotional reactions in this section have been taken for granted by many researchers, but there is a surprising dearth of empirical findings to support assumptions concerning the effects of compensation (see below).

2.7.1. *Acknowledgement and justice*

It is often asserted that granting state compensation is an attempt to acknowledge the suffering of victims of crime. As Dignan (2005, p. 44) notes it 'can be seen as a an embodiment of society's resolve to repair the harm that has been caused by an offence' and it 'serves symbolically to reforge (sic) the bonds that bind people together'. Until now evidence concerning the extent to which victims indeed feel the award acknowledges their victimisation is lacking.
The survey therefore queried the issue of acknowledgement. It is clear that recipients are of the opinion that the awards granted by the Dutch Fund serve this purpose (see table 2.22). 83% of respondents in this survey states they found the award to be an acknowledgement of their victimization. Only 7% of respondents disagreed.

Table 2.22: Effect of state compensation on acknowledgement of victim status (N=217)

The financial award of the Crime Compensation Fund made me feel acknowledged as a victim	
Completely disagree	1
Disagree	4
Slightly disagree	1
Neutral	10
Slightly agree	13
Agree	46
Completely agree	23
Do not know	2
Total	100%

State compensation may also grant victims a sense of justice. Similar to the observations concerning acknowledgement however, this function of awards has often been asserted but has not been fully researched. Erez & Tontodonato (1992) did show that the receipt of compensation increased the satisfaction with the whole of the criminal justice system, but did not differentiate between compensation from the offender or the state (see also Strang, 2002).

The present study reveals that a large majority of victims find the award from the Dutch state-run fund to be a form of justice. 80% of respondents agrees that this is the case. Table 2.23 reveals that only 6% of recipients disagrees.

Table 2.23: The experience of justice following an award (N=217)

Receiving a financial award from the Crime Compensation Fund was a form of justice to me	
Completely disagree	1
Disagree	2
Slightly disagree	3
Neutral	11
Slightly agree	16
Agree	38
Completely agree	26
Do not know	3
Total	100%

2.7.2. *Emotional support and coping*

In addition to its justice-related aspects, victims may also experience state compensation as a form of emotional support and this in turn may reduce their pain and suffering and enhance their ability to cope with their experiences.

It is apparent from the survey results that the majority of recipients experience the award to be a form of emotional support, see table 2.24. 75% of recipients agreed with the statement: 'Receing a financial award from the Crime Compensation Fund supported me emotionally', while only 13% disagreed.

Table 2.24: State compensation and emotional support (N=217)

Receiving a financial award of the Crime Compensation Fund supported me emotionally	
Completely disagree	2
Disagree	6
Slightly disagree	5
Neutral	12
Slightly agree	20
Agree	38
Completely agree	17
Do not know	2
Total	102%

Indeed the results reveal that recipients do not only experience emotional support through the Fund's awards, but that a majority even thinks the award reduced their pain and suffering. 61% of respondents agreed with the statement concerning this effect, while 23% disagreed (see table 2.25).

Table 2.25: Effect of state compensation on pain and suffering (N=217)

The financial award of the Crime Compensation Fund reduced my pain and suffering	
Completely disagree	5
Disagree	13
Slightly disagree	5
Neutral	13
Slightly agree	30
Agree	24
Completely agree	7
Do not know	2
Total	99%

In similar vein, a majority of recipients finds the award to have helped them cope with the consequences of their victimisation. As is apparent from table 2.26, 56% believes this to be the case, while 25% disagrees.

Table 2.26: State compensation and coping with victimisation (N=217)

Receiving a financial award from the Crime Compensation Fund helped me to cope with the aftermath of the crime	
Completely disagree	7
Disagree	13
Slightly disagree	5
Neutral	15
Slightly agree	25
Agree	22
Completely agree	9
Do not know	4
Total	100%

2.7.3. *Confirmation of innocence*

Many victims of crime blame themselves for the occurrence of crime (Janoff-Bulman, 1979). The feelings of guilt can weigh down heavily on victims of crime (Ehlers and Clark, 2000). An award from a state-run Compensation Fund may reduce or even remove feelings of self-blame and guilt, that victims may experience (Cobley, 1998). Indeed, 54% of the survey respondents found the award granted to them by the Dutch compensation fund to confirm their own innocence.

Table 2.27: State compensation: confirmation of innocence? (N=217)

Receiving a financial award from the Crime Compensation Fund confirmed my innocence	
Completely disagree	4
Disagree	8
Slightly disagree	4
Neutral	23
Slightly agree	9
Agree	28
Completely agree	17
Do not know	7
Total	100%

2.8. *Social value of money?*

The results of the survey repeatedly show that recipients of the Dutch Crime Compensation Fund perceive the grant as acknowledgement of their victimisation. It is however unclear whether victims know this acknowledgement is financed from public sources and subsequently whether they value the societal acknowledgement that this signals.

Table 2.28: Are recipients aware of the fact that the Fund awards victims public money? (N=217)

Knowledge about Fund's public function	Percentage of cases
No, I did not know the fund provided public money	36
Yes, I was aware of the fact that the fund provides public money	64
Total	100%

According to the survey results, two thirds of recipients know that the Dutch Crime Compensation Fund is publicly financed. However, 36% did not know that this was the case. Of those that did know, more than 75% valued the fact that the award signalled societal acknowledgement of their suffering. Only 15% did not agree (see table 2.29). Taken all together, almost half of recipients viewed the award as a social gesture, and consequently, more than half did not.

Table 2.29: Do recipients perceive the compensation granted by the Fund as a social gesture of solidarity and concern? (N=138)

Opinion	Percentage of cases
No, I did not	7
No, not really	8
Neutral	8
Yes, a little	11
Yes, I did	64
Don't know	2
Total	100%

2.9. *Summary*

The results reported in this chapter clearly indicate that the awards from the Dutch Crime Compensation Fund bear greater significance than just an increase of recipients' wealth. According to respondents receiving an award acknowledges their victimization (83%), provides them with a sense of justice (80%), and with emotional support (75%). It reduces their pain and suffering (61%), stimulates their coping process (56%) and confirms their own innocence (54%). The results provide empirical support to the assertions often voiced about the function of the state compensation.

3. Summary & conclusion

Crime compensation funds are schemes involved in "the granting of public funds to persons who have been victimized by a crime of violence and to persons who survived those killed by such a crime" (Edelhertz & Geis, 1974 as cited by Megret, 2010, p. 6). Many of these state-run schemes exist around the world (see O'Connell, 2003). Yet, little is known about the effects of state compensation. It is, for instance, unknown why victims apply for this type of compensation, which victims actually receive compensation, and how recipients perceive the money granted by crime compensation funds.

In order to fill this gap of knowledge, a survey was conducted among victims who received financial reparation from the Dutch Crime Compensation Fund in 2008. This chapter describes the survey's general results,[44] and provides, thereby, insight in recipients' characteristics, the procedure victims have to go through to be granted compensation, the compensation itself, and how recipients are affected by the compensation granted.

The Dutch Crime Compensation Fund grants compensation for economic losses (like lost income and medical expenses) and for non-economic losses (pain and suffering). On average, the Fund awards 3160 euro per victim (980 in economic compensation, and 2185 for pain and suffering). Seeing that the Fund is allowed to offer up to 31.800 euro (22.700 euro for economic losses and 9.100 for pain and suffering), its average awards appear rather low. Especially if one takes into account that close to half of the recipients did not receive any economic compensation or less than 100 euro's. Nevertheless, 75% of the respondents indicate to be satisfied with the award received. Moreover, one in three reports they expected to receive an even smaller award. Noteworthy is that victims' satisfaction with compensation closely resembles the extent to which the award meets or exceeds their expectations, rather than the absolute level of the award granted. Matching expectations with outcomes therefore seems a more important element of preventing dissatisfaction, then simply raising the amount awarded.

Looking at recipients' characteristics, it becomes apparent that victims who receive an award from the Dutch Crime Compensation Fund deviate from both victims of violent crime and the Dutch population as a whole. First of all, victims of severe violent crimes are overrepresented among recipients of state compensation. Secondly, recipients of state compensation generally fall into the lower income categories (which is in line with the Fund's safety net function). Thirdly, ethnic minorities seem to be underrepresented among recipients. Fourthly, victims of severe violent crime and female victims of crime are overrepresented in comparison with general victimization statistics. Unfortunately, the survey results do not provide solid explanations for these

44 Chapter 3 and 4 of this thesis provide in-depth analyses of the survey's results.

differences. The low number of ethnic minorities among respondents, for example, could either be due to their higher non-response rate in victimological surveys, or could signal that ethnic minorities face additional barriers in accessing the Fund. Same goes for the fact that relatively few men receive state compensation. Additional research is needed to investigate these matters.

According to the survey results most respondents know who their offender was (76%). Yet, only 8% received (partial) compensation from the culprit. Over half attempted to recoup their damages from the offender, but this fails in most cases.

Another noteworthy result is that recipients wait on average 20 months before they file an application with the Fund. That, while 89% reported the crime to police within a couple of days. What does explain the considerable amount of time between the victimization and an application with the fund is unclear. Possibly, victims prefer the criminal case to have run its course before going to the Crime Compensation Fund or is it that victims have to go through a long and arduous coping process before they are able to apply for compensation.

In general, recipients are positive about the Fund's application process. From a procedural justice perspective, it is clear that recipients believe the Fund's treatment is fair and respectful. Moreover, most victims are positive about the time lag between their application and the Fund's decision and the way the Fund informs them about its progress. However, recipients have fairly little knowledge about the way the Fund reaches it decisions, and a majority is referred to the Fund by Victim Support Netherlands. These results reveal shortcomings in the information provided to applicants.

The results reported in this chapter clearly indicate that the awards from the Dutch Crime Compensation Fund bear greater significance than just an increase of recipients' wealth. According to respondents receiving an award acknowledges their victimization (83%), provides them with a sense of justice (80%), and with emotional support (75%). It reduces their pain and suffering (61%), stimulates their coping process (56%) and confirms their own innocence (54%). The results provide empirical support to the assertions often voiced about the therapeutic function of the state compensation.

Finally, the survey results reveal that two thirds of recipients know that the Dutch Crime Compensation Fund is publicly financed. However, 36% did not know that this was the case. Of those who did know, more than 75% valued the fact that the award signalled societal acknowledgement of their suffering. Only 15% did not agree. Taken all together, almost half of recipients viewed the award as a social gesture, and consequently, more than half did not.

All and all, recipients seem to be overall content with the Dutch Crime Compensation Fund. They value the Fund's procedures, they are satisfied with its awards, and they feel acknowledged as victims by means of the money awarded by the Fund. However, The Fund could improve the way it provides information to victims in general and recipients in particular. For instance, how it decides on the amount of compensation to award, and about the fact that the Fund is publicly financed. After all, the Fund was initially established to show solidarity with the innocent victims of severe crimes (Ligterink & Hermsen, 2006), but 1/3 of the respondents indicated to have no knowledge about the state's involvement.

References

Cheon, A. & Regehr, C. (2006) Restorative justice models in cases of intimate partner violence: Revieweing the evidence. *Victims & Offenders*, 1(4), pp. 369-94.

Cobley, C. (1998). Financial compensation for victims of child abuse. *Journal of Social Welfare and Family Law, 20(3)*, p. 221-235.

Cosway, R. (1973). Crime compensation, 49 *Wash. L. Rev.* 551, pp. 551-70.

Dignan, J. (2005). *Understanding Victims and restorative justice*. Maidenhead, United Kingdom: Open University Press.

Dolan, P., Edlin, R., Tsuchiya, A., Wailoo, A., (2007), It ain't what you do, it's the way that you do it: Characteristics of procedural justice and their importance in social decision-making, *Journal of Economic Behavior and Organization*, 64, pp. 157-70.

Duff, P. (1998). The measure of criminal injuries compensation: political pragmatism or dog's dinner? *Oxford Journal of Legal Studies*, 18 (1), pp. 105-142.

Duff, P. (1995). Criminal injuries compensation: the symbolic dimension. *Juridical Review*, 40, 102.

Ehlers, A., & Clark, D.M. (2000). A cognitive model of posttraumatic stress disorder. *Behavior research and therapy*, 38, pp. 319-345.

Erez, E. & Tonado, P. (1996). Victim participation in sentencing and satisfaction with justice. *Justice Quarterly*, 9, pp. 393-415.

Feldthusen, B., Hankivsky, O. & Greaves, L. (2000). Therapeutic consequences of civil actions for damages and compensation claims by victims of sexual abuse. *Canadian Journal of Women and the Law*, 12, pp. 66-116.

Feskens, R.C.W. (2009). Difficult groups in survey research and the development of tailor made approach strategies. Heerlen/Voorburg. CBS.

Foa, E.B. & Rothbaum, B.O. (1998). Treating the Trauma of Rape: Cognitive-Behavioral Therapy for PTSD. New York, Guildford.

Fry, M. (1957). Justice for the Victims, The Observer (London), 7 july, 1957, at p. 8, col. 2. This article was subsequently republished in the Journal of Public Law: Margery Fry, Justice for Victims, 8 J PUB LAW 191 (1959). Justice for Victims, 8 *J PUB LAW* 191.

Groenhuijsen, M.S., & Pemberton, A. (2009). The EU framework decision for victims of crime: Does hard law make a difference? *European Journal of Crime, Criminal Law and Criminal Justice*, *17*(1), pp. 43-59.

Hanrath, J. (2002). *Slachtofferhulp en Culturele diversiteit*. Utrecht: Willem Pompe Instituut voor Strafrechtswetenschappen.

Hoogeveen & van Burik (2008): Doelgroep Schadefonds Geweldsmisdrijven. Een onderzoek naar de omvang en het profiel van de doelgroep van het Schadefonds Geweldsmisdrijven. Uitgegeven door Adviesbureau van Montfoort.

Janoff-Bulman, R. (1979). Characterological versus behavioral self-blame: Inquiries into depression and rape. *Journal of Personality and Social Psychology*, 37, pp. 1798 –1809.

Kalidien, S.N. & Eggen A.Th.J. (2009). *Crime and Law Enforcement 2008* (in Dutch: Criminaliteit en Rechtshandhaving 2008. Ontwikkelingen en samenhangen). The Hague: BJu. Research and policy 279.

Ligterink & Hermsen (2006). Schadefonds Geweldsmisdrijven "Het Schadefonds komt het slachtoffer tegemoet" Een institutioneel onderzoek naar Schadefonds Geweldsmisdrijven PERIODE: 1975 – 2005. Rapport Insitutioneel Onderzoek, 188. Koenen Baak en partners.

Lind, E.A. & Tyler, T.R. (1988), *The Social Psychology of Procedural Justice*. New York: Plenum Press.

Maercker, A. & Mullder, J. (2004). Social acknowledgement as a victim or survivor: a scale to measure a recovery factor of PTSD. *Journal of Traumatic Stress*, 17 (4), pp. 345–351.

Megret, F. (2010, forthcoming). Justifying Compensation by the International Criminal Court's Victims Trust Fund: Lessons from Domestic Compensation Schemes, *Brooklyn Journal of International Law*.

Miers, D. (2007) Looking beyond Great Britain: the development of criminal injuries compensation. In Walklate, S. (Ed.). *Handbook of Victims and Victimology*. Cullompton, UK; Willian Publishing.

Morris, T. (1961). Compensation for Victims of Crimes of Violence. *The Modern Law Review*, 24(6), pp. 744-747.

Mueller, G.O.W. (1965), Compensation for Victims of Crime: Thought before Action. 50 *Minn. L. Rev.* 213.

O'Connell, M. (2003). Criminal Injuries Compensation. Revisiting the rationale for state funded compensation for crime victims. Paper presented at the Innovation: Promising Practices for Victims and Witnesses in the Criminal Justice System – A National Conference, Canberra, 23 – 24 June, 2003.

Okimoto, T. G., & T.R. Tyler, (2007). Is compensation enough? Relational concerns in responding to unintended inequity. *Group Processes & Intergroup Relations*, 10(3), pp. 399-420.

Orth, U. (2003), Punishment goals of crime victims. *Law and Human behavior*, 27(2), pp. 173-186.

Pemberton, A. (2010a), Needs of victims of terrorism. In Letschert, R.M., Staiger, I., &

Pemberton, A. (eds.). Assisting victims of terrorism: Towards a European standard of justice. Dordrecht: Springer.
Pemberton, A. (2010b), The cross-over: An interdisciplinary approach to the study of victims of crime. Apeldoorn: Maklu.

Schultz, (1965). The violated: a proposal to compensate victims of violent crime, 10 *St. Louis U. L.J.* 238, pp. 238-250.

Silving, (1959). Compensation for victims of criminal violence. 8 *J Pub L.* 191, 236.

Sims, L. & Myhill, A. (2001). Policing and the public. Findings from the 2000 British Crime Survey. London: Home Office.

Strang, H. (2002) *Repair or revenge: victims and restorative justice*. Oxford: Oxford University Press.

Stutzer, A. & Frey, B.S. (2006), Political participation and procedural utility: An empirical study. *European Journal of Political Research*, 45, pp. 391–418.

Tyler, T. R. (1990). *Why people obey the law*. New Haven, USA: Yale University Press.

Tyler, T.R. (2006). Process Utility and Help Seeking: What Do People Want from Experts? *Journal of Economic Psychology*, 27, 360–376.

33 U. Chi. L. Rev. 531 (1965-1966) Compensation for Victims of Crime

Van Dijk, J.J.M., Manchin, R., van Kesteren, J.N. & Hideg, G. (2007). The Burden of Crime in the EU, A Comparative Analysis of the European Survey of Crime and Safety (EU ICS) 2005. Brussels, Gallup Europe.

Van Mierlo, F. & Pemberton, A. (2009). Van tevredenheid naar kwaliteit: een meetinstrument voor de slachtofferzorg. Tilburg: Intervict.

Wexler, D.B. & Wininck, eds., (1996). *Law in a therapeutic key; developments in the therapeutic jurisprudence*. Durham, North Carolina: Carolina Academic Press.

Wittebrood, K. (2006), *Slachtoffers en criminaliteit*. Den Haag; Sociaal en Cultureel Planbureau.

Young, M. (2003), *Meeting Victim Needs: What is the Role of Victim Compensation in Recovery?* Discussion Paper National Roundtable on Victim Compensation, National Center for Victims of Crime.

Appendix I: Questionnaire

Please note that the questionnaire provided to respondents was drafted in Dutch. Hence, the questions below are translated from the original survey. Although the translation was done with care by the author, it might be that due to differences in expressions, the translation slightly deviates from the original version.

Furthermore, the original questionnaire was written in a program designed for online questionnaires. Since that program was incompatible with text processing programs, like MS Word, it was not possible to copy the original layout.

Finally, the original questionnaire contained more questions than those translated below. Reason for not translating all questions is that some questions turned out to be of no use in the final analyses.

I. What is your nationality?

- Dutch
- Moroccan
- Turkish
- Surinam
- Dutch Antilles
- Aruban
- Other:
- Don't know

II. What is the highest level of education you have completed?

- Primary school
- Vmbo/mavo/mulo
- Havo/vwo/hbs/mms
- Mbo
- Hbo
- University
- Don't know

III. What was your disposable income at the time you filed an application at the Crime Compensation Fund?

(the disposable income is the amount of income left after taxes have been paid, available for spending and saving.)

- I had less than 10.000 euros a year to spend
- I had between 10 and 20.000 euros a year to spend
- I had between 20 and 30.000 euros a year to spend
- I had between 30 and 40.000 euros a year to spend
- I had more than 40.000 euro a year to spend
- Don't know

IV. Who informed you about the possibility of applying at the Dutch Crime Compensation Fund?

- The police
- Victim support
- A lawyer
- Family/friends
- TV/papers/magazines
- The internet
- Other:
- Don't know

V. What was the most important reason for you to file an application at the Dutch Crime Compensation Fund?

- @ answer
- Don't know

VI. How important were the following aspects to you, when you applied at the Dutch Crime Compensation Fund?

Please indicate whether you found them: Very unimportant, unimportant, fairly unimportant, not important/not unimportant,fairly important, important, very important, don't know

- Receiving financial compensation
- Being acknowledged as a victim
- Receiving emotional support
- Gerechtigheid bewerkstelligen
- Een bevestiging van onschuld krijgen
- Het misdrijf verwerken

VII. How much money did you expect to receive approximately when you filed an application at the Ducth Crime Compensation Fund?

- : @ euro
- Don't know

VIII. Was it clear to you how the Fund would determine whether you were eligible for compensation?

- Not at all
- Very little
- Neutral
- Somewhat
- To a great extent

IX. When you filed an application, did you then complete the application form yourself?

- No, someone else did it for me Go to question XIII.
- Yes, I completed the form myself

X. How much time did it take you to complete the forms (including the time you spend on looking up the necessary information))?

- : @ hours
- Don't know

XI. Did you think there were redundant questions you to answer on the application form?

- No
- Yes, some of the questions seemed redundant to me
- Yes, many questions seemed redundant to me
- Don't know

XII. Could you please indicate on a scale from 1 to 10 how stressful it was for you to fill in the application forms?

1= Not stressful at al
10= Very stressful.

XIII. How many times have you had contact with the Dutch crime compensation Fund? How many times did you, for example, receive a letter or a telephone call?

- : @ times
- Don't know

XIV. Do you think the Dutch Crime Compensation fund kept you well enough informed about the handling of your case?

- Not at all
- Very little
- Neutral
- Somewhat
- To a great extent
- Don't know

XV. How fair do you think the Dutch Crime Compensation Fund handled your case?

- Highly unfair
- Unfair
- Not unfair/not fair
- Fair
- Highly fair
- Don't know

XVI. Do you think the Dutch Crime Compensation Fund sufficiently reviewed the specific circumstances of your case?

- Not at all
- Very little
- Neutral
- Somewhat
- To a great extent
- Don't know

XVII. How many months were there between sending in the application form and receiving the compensation?

- : @ months
- Don't know

XVIII. What do you think about the time it took for the Fund to decide on your case? Did it go:

- Very slow
- Slow
- Not slow, nor quick
- Quick
- Very quick

XIX. Could you please indicate on a scale from 1 to 10 how stressful it was for you to fill in the application forms?

1= Not stressful at al
10= Very stressful.

XX. How much money did you receive **in total** from the Dutch Crime Compensation Fund?

- : @ euro
- Don't know

XXI. How satisfied were you with the total amount of money that you received from the Dutch Crime Compensation Fund?

- Very unsatisfied
- Unsatisfied
- Slightly unsatisfied
- Not unsatisfied/not satisfied
- Slightly satisfied
- Satisfied
- Very satisfied
- Don't know

XXII. Did the compensation you received match the expectations you had?

- No, I expected to receive **a lot more**
- No, I expected to receive **a little bit more**
- Yes, the compensation matched more or less my expectations
- No, I expected to receive **a little bit less**
- No, I expected to receive **a lot less**
- Don't know

XXIII. Did you receive compensation for pain and suffering?

- Yes, I did
- No I did not Go to question XXVI.
- Don't know Go to question XXVI.

XXIV. How much compensation did you approximately receive for pain and suffering?

- @ euro
- Don't know

XXV. How satisfied were you with the compensation for pain and suffering?

- Very unsatisfied
- Unsatisfied
- Slightly unsatisfied
- Not unsatisfied/not satisfied
- Slightly satisfied
- Satisfied
- Very satisfied
- Don't know

XXVI. Were you aware of the fact that the Crime Compensation fund is financed by the Dutch State, and that therefore you received public money?

- No, I did not Go to question XXVIII.
- Yes, I did

XXVII. Did you perceive it is an expression of the public's sympathy that you received compensation from the Dutch Crime Compensation Fund?

- No, I did not
- Not really
- Neutral
- Slightly
- Yes, I did
- Don't know

XXVIII. Were you aware that the Dutch Crime Compensation Fund is meant as a safety-net for those victims who are not able to receive compensation for their losses elsewhere?

- No, I was not
- Yes, I was
- Don't know

XXIX. Were you aware that the Crime Compensation Fund might demand repayment of the award if a victim receives compensation from the offender?

- No, I was not
- Yes, I was
- Don't know

XXX. Do you think it is just that the Crime Compensation Fund has the right to demand repayment?

- No, it is unjust, because: @
- Yes, it is just, because: @
- Don't know

XXXI. Please indicate whether you agree or disagree with the following statements by checking one of the following boxes:

Strongly agree, disagree, slightly disagree, neutral, slightly agree, agree, strongly agree, don't know

- The award of the Crime Compensation Fund reduced my pain and suffering
- The award of the Crime Compensation Fund made me feel acknowledged as a victim
- The award of the Crime Compensation Fund was a form of emotional support to me
- Receiving an award from the Crime Compensation Fund confirmed my innocence
- The award of the Crime Compensation Fund was a form of justice to me
- Receiving an award from the Crime Compensation Fund helped me to cope with the aftermath of the crime.
- Victims of crimes of violence are entitled to financial compensation.

XXXII. Did you know who the culprit if you victimization was?

- Yes
- No — Go to question XXXVI.
- Don't know — Go to question *Crime compensation Fund*

XXXIII. Did you try to recoup damages from the offender?

- Yes, I did
- No, I did not — Go to question XXXV.
- Don't know — Go to question *Crime compensation Fund*

XXXIV. Did you receive compensation form the offender?

- Yes, I did — Go to question *Crime compensation Fund*
- No, I did not — Go to question *Crime compensation Fund*
- Don't know — Go to question *Crime compensation Fund*

XXXV. Could you indicate why you choose not to recoup damages from the offender?

- The offender was a relative/an acquaintance
- The offender had no financial means
- I could not handle it emotionally
- I had no money for an attorney
- Different reason, namely:
- Don't know

XXXVI. If you would have known who the culprit was, would you then have tried to recoup damages from him/her?

- Yes, I would
- Probably, I would
- Probably I would not
- No, I would not
- Don't know

XXXVII. Could you please motivate this answer?

- : @
- Don't know

XXXVIII. Have you always been treaten with respect by the Crime Compensation Fund?

- Most definitely not
- Definitely not
- Not really
- Neutral
- Slightly
- Certainly
- Most certainly
- Don't know

XXXIX. When you look back at your application with the Crime Compensation fund, which feeling predominates (for example, gradetude, anger or a neutral feeling)?

- @:
- Don't know

XL. If you would become a victim of violent crime again, would you then apply for financial compensation with the Crime Compensation Fund too?

- Yes, I would Go to question XLII.
- I probably would Go to question XLII.
- I would probably not
- Don't know Go to question XLII.

XLI. Could you please indicate what would keep you from filing a claim again with the Crime Compensation Fund?

- An application takes too much time
- Amount of compensation is too low
- Application is too much of an emotional burden
- Different reason, namely:
- Don't know

XLII. Would you recommend other victims of violent crime to file a claim with the Crime Compensation Fund?

- Yes, I would
- Probably, I would
- Probably, I would not Go the question XLIV.
- No I would not Go to question XLIV.
- Don't know Go to question XLIV

XLIII. Could you motivate why you would recommend other victims to apply for compensation with the Crime Compensation Fund?

Please rank the reason you find most important with a 1. If you have several reasons, please rank the second most important reason with a 2, the third with a 3 and so forth.

- It is a easy way of getting your losses compensated
- Every victim is entitled to financial compensation
- It gives you acknowledgement as a victim
- It helps you cope with the aftermath of the crime
- Different reason, namely:
- Don't know

LV. You have reached the end of the survey. If you would like to elaborate on some of the answers you provided, or if there is something else you would like to share, please do so below.

Victims' satisfaction with compensation: how procedure matters

By J.D.W.E Mulder[45]

Introduction

If a person suffers harm as a result of a violent crime, one may decide to go to court and claim financial reparation from the offender. If one does, the question arises how to translate the victim's losses into a monetary equivalent. How to value the harm of a rape victim, for instance? Or that of someone victimized by domestic violence?

In finding damages, courts distinguish between economic and non-economic losses. In case of economic losses like lost wages and medical costs, courts compute market values and award damages accordingly (Cooter, 2003). No concrete guidance, however, is available to translate non-economic losses such as companionship, consort, sexual partnership, and affection, into appropriate monetary equivalents (Sunstein, 2008, p. 177).

Moore & Shepard (2006) have suggested that studies on victims' costs could facilitate determination of non-economic compensation levels. Over the years, various studies have been conducted to assess the losses, economic and non-economic, that victims of crime incur (see for example Cohen, 1988; Miller, Cohen & Rossman, 1993; Miller, Cohen, & Wiersema, 1996; Cohen, Rust, Steen & Tidd, 2004; Dolan, Loomes, Peasgood, & Tsuchiya, 2005; Atkinson, Healey & Mourato, 2005). The methods and results of these studies vary, yet Moore & Shepherd argue that the non-economic results provide rigorous means of determining financial reparation for pain and suffering (2006, p. 293).[46]

If we assume it is indeed possible to objectively assess the non-economic losses that victims suffer, and that courts will award damages accordingly, how would that affect those claiming compensation? Would it matter to

---

[45] José is grateful to Eric van Damme, Marc Groenhuijsen and Ben Vollaard for stimulating discussions and comments to earlier versions of this paper. And she feels obliged to mention that the title of this paper is inspired by that of Dolan et al (2007) on procedural justice: 'It ain't what you do, it's the way that you do it: Characteristics of procedural justice and their importance in social decision-making'.

[46] As explained by Groot et al. (2007), who study the costs of crime in the Netherlands, three steps have to be taken in order to determine the costs of crime: 1) which general costs does one include in the research, 2) which particular types of costs will be included (anticipatory costs, costs of the crime itself and/or costs in reaction to crime) and 3) which method will be used to determine costs. As scholars make different choices regarding these matters, their results have been found to vary significantly (Groot et al. 2007, p. x-xii).

victims whether or not their financial award equals the monetary value of their non-economic losses? A victim of rape, for instance, would she be satisfied with an amount of compensation equivalent to the U.S. $43.561 that Cohen calculated to be the amount of pain and suffering that the average rape victim incurs (1988, p. 547)?[47] Or would it require a lot more to 'repair' her non-economic losses?

To date many thousands of victims have received financial reparation for their losses. Yet, surprisingly little is known about victims' attitudes towards financial compensation. It is, for example, unknown how much victims expect to be awarded when they file for compensation, and how they feel about the amounts they eventually receive.

What is known, though, is that plaintiffs generally care about *how* outcomes are reached during a court case. The rich literature on procedural justice shows, for instance, that being able to ask questions and to experience polite and respectful treatment, contribute to an individual's well-being, irrespective of monetary outcomes (Lind & Tyler, 1988; Tyler, 2006: p. 374). Even in cases where disputes involve amounts of money up to U.S.$ 800.000, fair handling of cases has been proven to be more important to litigants than the actual outcome (Lind et al. (1993, as cited by Frey, Benz & Stutzer, 2004, p. 392). These findings raise the question whether procedural aspects are of importance to victims of violence who file for financial compensation too. Does it matter to them *how* they receive compensation? Or do they just care about the amount of money they receive? And how important is the monetary value of their losses?

In order to explore victims' perspectives on financial compensation, this paper presents the results of a study among recipients of the Dutch Crime Compensation Fund. This state-run fund offers financial compensation, economic and non-economic, to victims of violent crime. In total, 217 recipients replied to a survey on the Fund's awards and the procedure leading up to that. The survey was designed to assess how satisfied victims are with the compensation awarded to them and whether the amount received and/ or the Fund's procedure affects their (dis)satisfaction.

According to the results, recipients of the Dutch Crime Compensation Fund primarily receive compensation for their pain and suffering. Only half of the respondents received more than 100 euro's in compensation of their economic losses. With respectively €2070 and €1050, the average amounts of compensation for non-economic and economic losses appear modest. Nevertheless, 75% of the respondents is satisfied with the amount of money received.

---

[47] If we assume an annual depreciation rate of 2%, the pain and suffering of a rape victim would now entail 67.500 US dollar, or 53.500 euro.

Further statistical analysis indicates that satisfaction represents a complex concept. According to exploratory factor analysis one's satisfaction with compensation is closely related to several other variables. As a matter of fact, eight different questions concerning the respondent's encounter with the Fund coincide with each other and reflect just two broader concepts. These concepts could be interpreted as outcome satisfaction and procedural satisfaction.

How respondents scored on either of these factors was not affected by the amount of money that one had received. Nor was the respondent's income of any influence. Several procedural factors, however, did affect victim's outcome and procedural satisfaction. The number of times respondents were in contact with the Fund, for instance, and whether one perceived the Fund's procedure to be quick, positively influenced one's level of satisfaction.

All in all, no prove could be found that victims are concerned with the exact worth of their non-economic losses. As a matter of fact, financial matters seems of no importance at all. Instead, victims appear, just like other claimants, to be mainly affected by procedural matters.

The structure of the paper is as follows. Section 1 describes the study's design. It offers information on the Dutch Crime Compensation Fund, the respondents and the survey's methodology. Section 2 presents the survey's results and section 3 provides a short discussion.

1. *Methodology*

1.1. *The Dutch Crime Compensation Fund*

From the 1960's onwards, state-run crime compensation funds have been founded all over the globe.[48] The Dutch Crime Compensation Fund ('het Schadefonds Geweldsmisdrijven') is one of those funds. It was established in 1976 and falls under the responsibility of the Dutch minister of justice.[49]

The Fund offers financial support to victims of violent crimes. Consequently, victims of crimes like attempted homicide, rape, stalking and domestic violence, are entitled to file a claim with the Fund. From the moment a crime has been committed until three years after that, one is allowed to do so by

---

[48] New Zealand was the first to found a crime compensation Fund in 1963, Britain followed in 1964, and California and Wisconsin in 1965. Nowadays state compensation schemes operate in many countries, including Austria, Australia, Belgium, Bermuda, Canada, Columbia, Denmark, Germany, Finland, France, Hong Kong, Ireland, Israel, Italy, Japan, Luxembourg, the Netherlands, Northern Ireland, Norway, Philippines, Poland, Portugal, Scotland, Spain, Sweden, Switzerland, and United Arab Emirates (O'Connell, 2003).

[49] The fund is financed through general tax revenues. For more information about the fund see: www.schadefonds.nl/en_GB/algemeen/

means of a written application form.[50] Once approved, the Fund awards either economic compensation (for economic losses like medical expenses and lost income), non-economic compensation (to cover pain and suffering), or both.[51] The amount of economic compensation depends on the costs incurred – up to a maximum of 22.700 euro. Compensation for pain and suffering is determined by use of 8 scales, ranging from 550 to 9.100 euro.[52]

Noteworthy is that during its proceedings, the Fund does not show any relational concern. For example, the Fund does not try to appease the victim, or to acknowledge the harm that has been caused (e.g. Okimoto & Tyler, 2007). Nor does the Fund endorse the government's involvement.

1.2. *The study*

The current study is part of a larger explorative study into the effects of financial compensation (see Mulder, 2009a, 2009b, 2010). Participants were recruited through the Dutch Crime Compensation Fund in the spring of 2009. In total, 1000 victims were approached to fill out a survey concerning the financial compensation they had received in 2008, and the procedure leading up to that.[53] 217 recipients returned a copy that was usable for analysis (out of 225). Furthermore, the Fund provided additional information from their files.

In order to explore victims' attitudes towards financial compensation, the survey covered the following topics[54]:

- The compensation received: the exact amounts of economic and non-economic compensation transferred by the Fund to respondents. Regarding these numbers, recipients were asked to state their satisfaction with the total amount of compensation received and with that for pain and suffering.[55] Furthermore, recipients were asked to report whether the total award had matched their expectations or not.

---

50 If one does not have knowledge about the Fund's existence or another solid reason for not applying within three years after the crime has been committed, the Fund will decide on the application anyway.

51 The Fund does not apply strict rules concerning evidence of harm. Victims simply have to provide a convincing story. However, one's credibility is of course enhanced if the application form contains the copy of a police report or medical information.

52 A standardized list of physical injuries plus an evaluation of the nature, circumstances, and consequences of the crime determines the level of non-economic compensation that the Fund awards (see Schadefonds Geweldsmisdrijven, 2007).

53 In 2008 a total of 4459 victims was granted compensation by the Dutch Crime Compensation Fund.

54 As described in chapter 2 of this thesis, the survey covered several topics. Here only the ones relevant to procedural matters are mentioned. The complete survey can be found in the appendix of chapter 2.

55 In order to keep the number of survey questions as limited as possible, respondents were not questioned separately about economic compensation.

- The Fund's procedures: the survey contained several questions regarding the Fund's procedures. Reason for doing so is the rich literature on procedural justice which shows that plaintiffs do not only care about the outcome of a trial, but also care deeply about the process by which conflicts are resolved and decisions are made (Lind & Tyler, 1988; Tyler, 2006: p. 374). More specific, the following three factors have been shown to be of importance: 1) respectful and fair treatment, 2) information concerning the process and outcome of their cases, and 3) possibilities for participation (Strang, 2002). Hence, the survey queried various procedural aspects. For example, respondents' knowledge concerning the Fund's decision making process and whether victims themselves had applied, or if someone else had done so on their behalf. Moreover, victims were questioned about the length of the procedure, the number of times they had been in contact with the Fund, whether they thought they were well enough informed about the Fund's proceedings, and whether the Fund had treated them with respect.

1.3. *Sample*

All respondents to the survey were victims of crimes of violence. One in four, for example, was victim of a (severe) sexual crime and one in ten victim of severe physical abuse. Table 1.1 provides an overview.

Table 1.1: Types of crime suffered by respondents (N=217)

Type of crime	percentage of respondents*
Homicide and manslaughter	1
Attempted homicide and manslaughter	7
Severe sexual crimes**	15
Sexual crimes***	9
Violent theft	24
Assault and battery	24
Severe assault ***	11
Threat*****	7

* Because of rounding, the total does not add up to 100

** among others: rape, involuntarily prostitution, intercourse with someone under the age of 12

*** among others: fornication, (attempted) sexual violation

**** among others: hostage taking, kidnapping and severe physical abuse

***** among others: extortion, stalking

The sample consisted of 217 victims, of which approximately half were female (52%). Average age at the time of application was 38 years (range

0-88, sd=19).[56] Respondents' level of income was relatively low: 65% had a disposable income of less than 20.000 euro a year.[57]

A majority (54%) had filled out the Fund's application form themselves. Lawyers or victims' assistance did so for the remaining 46%. On average, it had taken the Fund two months to decide on an application (see table 1.2). Four in ten recipients thought the completion of their case went (very) quick, while almost two in ten (19%) indicated it took a (very) long time.

Table 1.2: Fund's processing time (N=217)

	Number of days
Mean	89
Std. Deviation	53
Minimum	3
Maximum	304

Finally, not all respondents were aware of the fact the Dutch Crime Compensation Fund offers public money to victims of violent crime. 64% did have this knowledge, while 36% did not (see table 1.3).[58]

Table 1.3: Respondents knowledge about Fund's public function (N=217)

Knowledge about Fund's public function	Percentage
No, I did not know the Fund provided public money	36
Yes, I was aware of the fact that the Fund provides public money	64
Total	100

1.3.1. *Non-response*

Whilst the sample of respondents cannot be taken as representative of the Fund's recipients as a whole, there is no reason to believe it is atypical. A comparison of the sample (N=217) with the total group of recipients approached for participation (N=1000), shows resemblance on aspects like gender, age, type of crime and compensation (see table 1.4).

---

[56] Most respondents were between the age of 15 and 25 (29%), which is in line with the fact that young people run the highest risk of falling victim to crime (see chapter 2 of this thesis).

[57] 36% of the respondents indicated to have a disposable income of less than 10.000 euro a year, which is rather low compared to the fact that only 5% of all Dutch citizens has less than 10.000 euro to spend annually. Moreover, 29% of the respondents indicated to have an income of 10-20.000 euro, while only 25% of the Dutch population has such an income.

[58] More information about the sample can be found in chapter 2 of this thesis.

Table 1.4: Comparison of respondents and total pool of recipients approached for participation.

	Gender	Average age	Percentage severe crime*	Percentage less severe crime*	Length of procedure (in days)	Average amount non-economic compensation	Average amount total compensation
Respon-dents	52% female	38 (SD=19)	35%	65%	89 (sd=53)	2140 euro (sd=1445)	3120 euro (sd= 3064)
Recipients approached	53% female	36 (SD=17)	32%	68%	92 (sd=56)	2130 euro (sd=1500)	3080 euro (sd=2800)

* Severe crime consists of homicide & manslaughter, attempted homicide & manslaughter, severe sexual crimes and severe assault. Less severe crime on the other hand, consists of sexual crimes, violent theft, assault and battery and threat.

2. *Results*

2.1. *Compensation*

The average respondent to the survey received an amount of 1050 euro to cover economic losses and 2070 euro for pain and suffering. Hence, in total the average respondent received 3120 euro.

As could be expected, awards for pain and suffering varied considerably per type of crime: victims of more severe crimes received larger awards than victims of less severe crimes (see table 2.1). Respondents who had fallen victim to severe sexual crimes, for example, received 3570 euro on average, while victims of threat received only half of that (1650 euro).

Furthermore, compensation for pain and suffering varied among victims who suffered the same type of crime; several victims of violent theft, for instance, received the minimum award of 550 euro's while others received more than 4000 euro (see table 2.1). Nevertheless, victims of more severe crimes received higher awards of non-economic compensation than victims of less severe crime did (chi-square=25.133, df=6, N=217, $p<.001$).

Whereas almost all respondents received non-economic compensation, close to one in four did not receive any economic compensation at all. Another 20% was granted less than 100 euro. Hence, for almost one in two recipients compensation for pain and suffering was all, or close to all, they received.[59]

59 If one takes into account that many types of economic losses are covered by private or social insurance schemes, it is not surprising that relatively few respondents received economic compensation. Medical expenses and lost income, for example, are in the Netherlands primarily paid for by obligatory, social, insurance schemes. Moreover, the Dutch insurance market is notably large; every citizen spends yearly no less than 4600 euro on different insurance policies (CEA Statistics, 2009).

Those who did received economic compensation, were granted 1370 euro (N=167; sd=2800 euro) on average. If we exclude victims who received less than 100 euro's, the average amount rises to 1850 (N=122; sd=3150 euro). Per type of crime, no significant differences appear ($r_{jonkheere\text{-}terpstra}$ = 0,121, ns). Surviving next of kin receive noteworthy high amounts of economic compensation though; 3880 euro on average.

Table 2.1: Average awards in euro's per type of crime, minimum and maximum awards and standard deviation (n=217)

Type of crime	Average award pain & suffering	Min-max (sd) pain & suffering	Average total award	Min-max (sd) total award
Homicide and manslaughter	0*	0-0 (0)*	3880	2100-5150 (1600)
Attempted homicide and manslaughter	2550	550-5500 (1610)	3700	550-9970 (2900)
Severe sexual crimes	3570	550-5750 (1200)	4500	710-13620 (2200)
Sexual crimes	1850	350-4150 (1250)**	2900	350-14075 (3100)
Violent theft	2150	550-8250 (1400)	2750	550-17850 (2800)
Assault and battery	1400	550-5500 (1150)	2500	550-23420 (3450)
Severe assault	2000	375-5500 (1350)**	3700	90-17225 (4150)
Threat	1650	550-5500 (700)	2200	570-5855 (1400)
Total	2070	350-8250 (1500)**	3120	90-23420 (3050)

* Non-economic compensation equals zero here, as surviving next of kin are not entitled to compensation for pain and suffering under Dutch law.

** The minimum amount of non-economic compensation awarded is sometimes lower than 550 euro, if the victim is considered partly responsible.

2.2. *Expectations*

How much compensation did victims expect to receive when they filed for compensation? Did they anticipate to receive millions? Or were their expectations more or less in line whit what they received?

In answer to the question 'how much compensation did you expect to receive when you filed your application?' a majority of respondents (60%) checked the do-not-know box. Of those who did mention a specific number, 50% thought they would be awarded an amount ranging from 0 to 1500 euro's and 36% expected an award of 1500 up to 5000 euro. The remaining 15% anticipated an award of 5000-50.000 euro.

In the light of these results it is not surprising that, as Table 2.2 reveals, more than one in three respondents (36%) indicated that the total amount of compensation turned out to be (much) higher than they had hoped for. For more than one in four the total award was (slightly) less than what was expected. Noteworthy is that here too a significant amount of respondents (24%) checked the do-not-know box. Apparently, victims do not always have a concrete idea of how much money they expect to receive when they file for compensation.

Table 2.2: Did the total award meet the recipients' expectations (N=217)?

The award was...	Percentage
Much lower than expected	12
Slightly lower than expected	15
Equal to what was expected	13
Slightly higher than expected	16
Much higher than expected	20
Do not know	24
Total	100%

2.3. *Are recipients satisfied with the Fund's awards?*

Seeing that the Fund's awards are more or less in line with what victims hoped to receive, one might expect victims to be satisfied with the compensation granted to them. But are they? In order to study victims' satisfaction, respondents were asked to indicate on a 7-point scale how satisfied they were with both the total amount received, and that for pain and suffering.[60]

75% of the respondents answered to the question 'How satisfied were you with the total amount of money that you received from the Dutch Crime Compensation Fund?' to be rather to highly satisfied. A similar number said so about the non-economic award. Less than 15% was more or less dissatisfied (see Table 2.3).

[60] See footnote 9.

Table 2.3: Satisfaction with non-economic compensation (N=156) and total compensation (N=217), in percentages

	Non-economic compensation	Total award
Highly dissatisfied	4	6
Dissatisfied	2	7
Rather dissatisfied	7	4
Neither dissatisfied or satisfied	8	6
Rather satisfied	14	13
Satisfied	39	35
Highly satisfied	19	27
Don't know	6	2
Total	100%	100%

2.3.1. *Why are victims satisfied?*

In order to explain the high levels of satisfaction, several factors have been explored. First of all, the interaction between satisfaction and the amount of compensation received. After all, it seems valid to assume that the more one receives, the more satisfied one is. The survey results, however, do not show any prove for this hypothesis: there is no indication of a statistical relation between recipients' satisfaction and amount of money received (see Table 2.4).

Secondly, compared to the disposable income of the general Dutch population, respondents' income level is rather low; for 65% of the respondents the average award of 3120 euro yields at least 16% of their yearly income (as that is 20.000 euro or less). Could it be that one is satisfied with the Fund's grants just because it equals a considerable part of one's wealth? As shown by Table 2.4, there is no such relationship either: recipients with lower disposable incomes are not more satisfied than those with higher incomes, or vice versa (see Table 2.4).[61]

[61] According to several statistical tests, income groups do not diverge from each other, nor from respondents in general. Respondents with a lower incomes, for example, did not suffer more or less severe crimes than did respondents with higher incomes (c^2: 6.459, df=4, N=185, ns). Nor did they receive more or less compensation (total compensation: Kruskal Wallis H(5)= 5.066, p>.05,ns; non-economic compensation: Kruskal Wallis H(5)= 5.066, p>.05,ns). Ordinal regression analysis confirms these results. Respondents' satisfaction could not be predicted by means of income, type of crime suffered, and compensation received: (R^2=.03 (Hosmer & Lemeshow), .094 (Cox & Snell), .097 (Nagelkerke). Model $c^2(12)$=17.781, p>.05, ns.)

Table 2.4: Statistical relations between satisfaction with received awards and six outcome-related variables

Related variables	Statistical relation
Satisfaction with total award and total amount of compensation received	H (6)=11.197, ns
Satisfaction with non-economic award and amount of non-economic compensation received	H (6)= 9.640, ns
Satisfaction with total award and victims' disposable income	c^2: 5.021 (2), N=179, ns.
Satisfaction with non-economic award and victims' disposable income	c^2: 2.752 (2), N=125, ns.
Satisfaction with total award and whether compensation matched expectations	c^2=47.726 df=2, $p<.01$ Somers D=.495
Satisfaction with non-economic award and whether compensation matched expectations	Fischer's exact test=20,102, $p<.01$; Somer's D=0.501

Thirdly, we have seen how the Fund's awards are more or less in line with what victims hoped to receive. One might, therefore, expect victims to be satisfied with the compensation granted to them. As shown in Table 2.4, this is indeed the case: recipients whose expectations were below or equal to the Fund's award, are those who are satisfied. Conversely, victims who were expecting more than what they received are the ones less satisfied. Hence, one's expectations appear to influence one's level of satisfaction.

What do these results tell us? Is it valid to conclude that from the recipients' perspective there is no need to increase compensation levels, as there is no relation between compensation levels and satisfaction? And that, instead, the Fund should provide better information to (potential) claimants about what to expect? Or should we be cautious to draw any conclusions from these results? Lerner (2003) points us in the direction of the latter. He, after all, explains that when people are asked to state how they feel about different aspects of an encounter with a specific authority, the answers to these different aspects may just reflect the respondents' attitude towards the authority in general (2003).

In this case, recipients who are generally satisfied with the Crime Compensation Fund, might have responded generally positive to the survey questions . The other way around, people less satisfied or even dissatisfied with the Fund, might have given less positive or negative answers. As a result, recipients' level of satisfaction and the variable that reflects how the awards matched one's expectations might just be a reflection of their attitude towards the Fund in general. If so, the survey variables cannot be treated as independent, nor is it valid to explore their relationship to other variables -as we did earlier, see Table 2.4-.

Hence, in order to interpret the results presented in Table 2.4, we need to determine whether there is a general construct that underlies the respondents' answers. An exploratory factor analysis provides the means to do so. After all, this widely used statistics tool helps to detect possible structures in the relationships between variables (Kline, 1994).[62] The upcoming paragraph describes how such analysis was performed for eight of the survey variables.

2.4. *What does satisfaction actually entail?*

In order to ascertain whether a general construct underlies the respondents' answers to the survey, all variables that could be the reflection of such a construct were selected. Table 2.5 provides an overview of these variables and the questions they were based upon.

Table 2.5: Variables selected for the exploratory factor analysis[63]

1 *Knowledge of application process* Was it clear to you how the Crime Compensation Fund would determine whether you were eligible for compensation? (5 possible answers ranging from 'Not at all' to 'To a great extent')
2 *Respectful treatment* Have you always been treated with respect by the Crime Compensation Fund? (7 possible answers ranging from 'Most definitely not' to 'Most certainly')
3 *Adequately informed* Do you think the Crime Compensation Fund kept you well enough informed about the handling of your case? (5 possible answers ranging from 'Not at all' to 'To a great extent')
4 *Fair handling of cases* How fair do you think the Crime Compensation Fund handled your case? (5 possible answers ranging from 'Highly unfair' to 'Highly fair')
5 *Specific circumstances taken into account* Do you think the Crime Compensation Fund sufficiently reviewed the specific circumstances of your case? (5 possible answers ranging from 'Not at all' to 'To a great extent')

62 It does so by assessing which variables cluster together in a meaningful way: the statistical program looks for variables that correlate highly with a group of other variables but do not with variables outside that group (See Appendix A).

63 As explained in more detail in de Appendix, initially two more variables were examined for underlying constructs. Yet, since their communalities were lower than .5, the variables based on the questions: 'Do you think there were unnecessary questions you had to answer on the application form' and 'How would you rate the time you had the wait for the decision of the Fund', were excluded from the final model.

6 *Satisfaction with total compensation* How satisfied were you with the total amount of money that you received from the Crime Compensation Fund? (7 possible answers ranging from 'Very unsatisfied' to 'Very satisfied')
7 *Compensation matched expectations* Did the compensation you received match the expectations you had? (5 possible answers ranging from 'I expected to receive a lot more' to 'I expected a lot less')
8 *Satisfaction with pain and suffering award* How satisfied were you with the compensation for pain and suffering? (7 possible answers ranging from 'Very unsatisfied' to 'Very satisfied')

As all the selected variables were measured on a Likert scale, which cannot be presumed to be linear, variables had to be transformed by means of a categorical principal component analysis (CATPCA) prior to the exploratory factor analysis (see Linting et al., 2007).[64] Subsequently, it was possible to perform an orthogonal exploratory factor analysis, with varimax rotation and Kaiser normalization. Table 2.6 shows the results.[65]

64 This method is the nonlinear equivalent of standard principal component analysis. It reduces the observed variables into a number of uncorrelated principal components and then assigns numeric values through a process called optimal quantification (also referred to as optimal scaling, or optimal scoring) (see Linting, 2007).

65 A orthogonal rotation was chosen to report, as the oblimin rotation showed that both components can be seen as independent (r_s=-0,082, ns). Due to the relatively small sample size (<250), only factors that load more than 0.450 are reported. The Kaiser-Meyer-Olkin measure verified sampling adequacy for the analysis, KMO=0.797 (good/great according to Field, 2009) and all KMO values for individual items were >0.606, which is well above the acceptable limit of 0.5. Bartlett's test of sphericity (chi square (28)= 626,906, p<0.01), indicated that correlations between items were sufficiently large for PCA. Several initial analyses were run to obtain these results. Primarily, three components had eigenvalues over Kaiser's criterion of 1 and in combination explained 57% of the variance. The scree plot was ambiguous and showed inflexions that would justify retaining just 2 components. Due to low communalities two variables were excluded (1: do you think there were unnecessary questions you had to answer on the application form; 2: How would you rate the time you had the wait for the decision of the Fund). The two remaining components explain 61% of the variance. According to the CATPCA analysis, Crombach's alpha = .908, so we can assume the overall reliability of the items is good (alpha>0.8 are good according to Field, p. 681). Appendix A offers additional information.

Table 2.6: Results of the orthogonal exploratory factor analysis (N=217)

	Component	
	1	2
1 Knowledge of application process		0,738
2 Respectful treatment		0,705
3 Adequately informed		0,601
4 Fair handling of cases	0,772	
5 Specific circumstances taken into account	0,780	
6 Satisfaction with total amount of compensation	0,854	
7 Compensation matched expectations	0,810	
8 Satisfaction with pain and suffering award	0,632	

Clearly, there is redundancy in the variables; all eight variables cluster onto two components. Apparent is how highly the variables load onto the components; correlations between the variables and factors range from .601 till .854 (see Table 2.6). This implies the factors explain 36% up to 73% of the variance in the variables, which is considered a good result (Croon, 2006).[66] Moreover, the components jointly account for a significant proportion (61%) of the variance in the transformed variables.

The fact that all variables load highly onto the factors, tells us that the variables do not reflect eight independent aspects of a recipient's encounter with the Crime Compensation Fund. Instead, they provide information about two general constructs. Interpretation of these general constructs largely depends on the variables with the highest factor loadings, as these are considered to be the most important (Croon, 2006; Kline 1994).[67] An appropriate label for factor 1's therefore needs to reflect 'satisfaction with total amount of compensation' (loading of .854) and that for component 2: 'knowledge of application process' (loading of .738).

Yet, since the correlation coefficients of other variables are relatively high as well, it seems valid to take other variables into account too. In case of factor 2 all variables can be interpreted as a reflection of a victim's feelings regarding the Fund's *procedure*. After all, the variables concern the adequacy of information and whether respondents are treated with respect. These variables are considered two of the three basic components of procedural

---

66 Loadings of +- .5 or greater are considered practically significant, loadings exceeding .7 are considered indicative of well-defined structure. Moreover, loading of .8 and above are viewed as extremely high (Croon, 2006, p. 64).

67 Statistics programs do not assign labels to the factors it distracts during factor analysis. Therefore, interpretation of the factors' labels is left up to the researcher's discretion (Croon, 2006; Kline, 1994).

justice (Strang, 2003). Hence, 'procedural satisfaction' appears to be an appropriate label for factor 2.

In case of factor 1, 'outcome satisfaction' seems to be a valid label. After all, the variable with the highest loading is 'satisfaction with total amount of compensation', which provides information about the actual outcome, just like 'compensation matched expectations' and 'satisfaction with pain and suffering award' do. At first sight, the variables 'fair handling of cases' and 'specific circumstances taken into account', seem less obvious elements of this construct. Yet, as both variables correlate highly to the factor (respectively .772 and .780)[68], they do contribute significantly to the construct. A reasonable explanation might be that while answering the question: 'how fair do you think the Crime Compensation Fund handled your case', victims considered the fairness of the Fund's *award*. And that the question: 'do you think the Crime Compensation Fund sufficiently reviewed the specific circumstances of your case', triggered recipients to assess whether the Fund's *award* was appropriate considering their specific circumstances.

In sum, Lerner's thesis on how one should be careful when analyzing respondents' reports of an encounter with a specific authority, is of concern here too. Eight different questions about the victim's encounter with the Dutch Crime Compensation did not result in eight independent measures; instead they reflect just two broader concepts. Hence, the statistical relations revealed in Table 2.4 do not present any reliable insights. As a result, we cannot conclude that recipients whose expectations were below or equal to the Fund's award, are those who are satisfied, - as we did earlier-. Nor can we conclude that form a recipients' perspective, compensation levels should not be raised. Instead, if we want to understand why recipients are satisfied or why they are not, the constructs 'outcome satisfaction' and 'procedural satisfaction' have to studied in closer detail. In the upcoming paragraphs, we will do so.

2.4.1. *Again: Why are recipients satisfied?*

Now we know that recipients' satisfaction consists of an outcome and a procedural component, we can explore explanations for why some victims are satisfied and others are not.

Let's start with 'outcome satisfaction'. Seeing that an application with the Crime Compensation Fund results in a financial award, it seems straightforward to assume that recipients' outcome satisfaction correlates with the amount of compensation received. After all, compensation is the outcome here.

---

[68] See footnote 21.

Table 2.7: Correlations between the two satisfaction factors and four outcome-related variables

	1	2	3	4	5	6
1 Factor 1_outcome satisfaction	1,000					
2 Factor 2_procedural satisfaction	-,082	1,000				
3 Compensation for pain and suffering	,100	,090	1,000			
4 Total amount of compensation	,066	,145	,785**	1,000		
5 Total compensation/yearly disposable income	-,043	,130	,617**	,742**	1,000	
6 Compensation for pain and suffering/yearly disposable income	,010	,059	,743**	,535**	,860**	1,000

** Spearman correlation significant at .01 level

As Table 2.7 shows, respondents who received relatively high amounts of compensation are not more satisfied with the outcome than those who received relatively little. Nor is it the case that victims with lower levels of disposable income are more satisfied about the outcome than victims with higher levels are (H(4)=2.882, ns). The ratio of one's income and the received award does not provide any information about one's satisfaction either (see Table 2.7). In other words, the survey results do not show any sign of a significant relation between respondents' outcome satisfaction and the actual outcome.
Regression analysis confirms these results; knowing how much compensation one received and what his income was, does not help to predict a respondent's satisfaction with outcome (R^2 of the model is .05, so only 5% of the variation in outcome satisfaction can be explained by means of these variables).

Another explanation for outcome satisfaction might be respondents' awareness of the State's involvement with the Fund. After all, various scholars have argued that the mere fact of receiving public money, serves as a "therapeutically symbolic gesture of collegiality and concern" (Freckelton, 2004, p. 58-9). The results, however, do not show any evidence in this direction. Recipients who knew the Fund is run by the Dutch state, do not report significantly more, or less, outcome satisfaction than do recipients who do not know about the state's involvement (H(2)=-.428, ns).

Actually, the only significant relation that could be determined was that between outcome satisfaction and the amount of time it had taken the Fund to decide on a case. The more time the Fund had needed, the less satisfied recipients are (r_s=-.137 $p<.05$). An even stronger relation appears between outcome satisfaction and how recipients' anticipated the Fund's processing time. Respondents who thought the Fund's proceedings went fairly quick, were much more satisfied about the outcome than respondents who felt it had taken a (very) long time ($r_{jonkheere\text{-}terpstra}$ =.392, p<.01).[69] This result is confirmed by regression analysis: if we know whether respondents indicated the Fund's processing time as very quick, quick, not slow or quick, slow or very slow, 24% of the variance in outcome satisfaction can be explained, which is considered a good result (Field, 2009).[70]

2.4.2. *Procedural satisfaction*

The previous paragraph showed us how the actual outcome of an application with the Crime Compensation Fund, does not affect respondents' outcome satisfaction. Does the same go for procedural satisfaction? Or do procedure aspects affect one's level of procedural satisfaction to a great extant?

Let us start with analyzing the effect of victims' participation on procedural satisfaction. It has been shown that, from a procedural justice perspective, it is beneficial to victims to participate in their case (Tyler, 1990). Does this imply that respondents who filled out the application form themselves are more satisfied about the procedure? Or could it be that these respondents are actually less satisfied, as increased participation might lead to psychological stress (Pemberton, 2010a, p. 79; Cheon & Regehr, 2006)?

According to the statistical analysis, the respondents who filled out the forms themselves (N=117), are significantly more satisfied about the procedure than those who did not (U= 4592, Z=2.745, N=217, 2-tailed, p<.01, r=0.186).[71] In other words, participation does seem to increase procedural satisfaction. Yet, satisfaction does depend on how one valued the application form; recipients who thought the form contained (many) unnecessary questions, were less satisfied about the procedure than recipients who said only a few questions were unnecessary (H(2)= 8.626, p<.01, J= 1178, Z=2.717, $r_{Jonckheere\text{-}Terpstra}$= -.277).

Another variable that concerns victims' participation, or perhaps more in particular the way victims are informed about the process and outcome of their cases, is the number of times recipients have been in contact with

---

69 Noteworthy is how respondents seems to have a rather good sense of how long it had taken the Fund to decide on their case; the correlation coefficient between their estimates and the actual time it had taken the Fund was .630.

70 Predicting outcome satisfaction by means of the dummy variable 'did the procedure went quick or slow', resulted in a model in which R equals .489, R^2=.239, p<.001. Both the constant and beta differed significantly from zero (p<.001).

71 Statistical tests showed that respondents who filled out the application forms themselves, did not diverge from respondents who asked others to do so. There were no differences in type of crime that one had suffered, for instance (c^2: 7.521, df=7, N=217, ns). Nor were there differences in compensation (total compensation: Mann Whitney U= 5384, Z=-.242, N=217, 2-tailed, ns; non-economic compensation: U= 5692,Z=-.361, N=217, 2-tailed, ns). Level of income did not differ too (c^2: 9.249, df=4, N=217, ns).

the Fund. According to respondents, this number varies between 0 and 10. In other words, some victims speak to or correspond with the Fund quite frequently, while others just apply and wait for the Fund's decision without any further contact. It turns out that the more contact one has, the more satisfied one is about the procedure ($H(9)= 34.803$, $p<.01$, $J=9369$, $Z=4.962$, $r_{Jonckheere\text{-}Terpstra} = .369$).

Another likely factor influencing recipients' procedural satisfaction seems to be the amount of time it takes the Fund to decide on a case. After all, the less time it takes, the quicker the case is closed and the sooner one receives compensation. However, the data does not provide evidence for such an association, the correlation coefficient is even particularly low ($r_s=.004$).

How victims feel about the amount of time it takes the Fund to decide, though, is of statistical significance. Recipients who are positive about the time lag between application and decision, are more satisfied about the procedure than are those who regard the Fund's processing to be slow ($H(4)=26.627$, $p=.002$; $r_{Jonckheere\text{-}Terpstra}=.328$).

So procedural factors do affect recipients' procedural satisfaction. Financial aspects, on the other hand, do not affect procedural satisfaction. As shown in Table 2.7, the amount of compensation one receives, is not related to the one's level of procedural satisfaction.

Finally, the data show that knowledge about the Dutch state's involvement with the Fund is correlated with procedural satisfaction. Victims who are aware of the Fund's public function are significantly more satisfied than those who are not ($U= 3831$, $Z=-3.641$, $p<.01$; $r=.247$).

Table 2.8: Statistical associations between procedural satisfaction and several procedural variables

Variables	Association between variables
Procedural satisfaction and filling in application form	Positive: $U= 4592$, $Z=2.745$, $N=217$, 2-tailed, $p<.01$, $r=0.186$
Procedural satisfaction and amount of unnecessary questions	Negative: $H(2)= 8.626$, $p<.01$, $J= 1178$, $Z=2.717$, $r_{Jonckheere\text{-}Terpstra}= -.277$
Procedural satisfaction and amount of contact with Fund	Positive: $H(9)= 34.803$, $p<.01$, $J=9369$, $Z=4.962$, $r_{Jonckheere\text{-}Terpstra}= .369$
Procedural satisfaction and knowledge about Fund's public function	Positive: $U= 3831$, $Z=-3.641$, $p<.01$; $r=.247$
Procedural satisfaction and whether process went quick or slow	Negative: $H(4)=26.627$, $p=.002$; $r_{Jonckheere\text{-}Terpstra}=.328$

Regression analysis shows that the combination of the amount of contact recipients have and whether victims regard the process as quick or slow, provides the best clues to whether a recipient will be satisfied with the procedure or not; together they explain 29% of the variance in procedural satisfaction.[72]

3. Discussion and conclusion

Victims of violent crime may file for financial reparation in order to compensate their losses. Many victims have done so through the years and significant amounts of money have been awarded to them. Yet, it has remained unknown how recipients perceive financial compensation. How important is the amount of compensation, for example, and do other non-financial factors matter (as well)?

The present paper expounds the results of a survey held among 217 victims of violent crime who received financial compensation from the Dutch Crime Compensation Fund. This state-run fund is established to offer financial reparation to victims of violence. Put differently, the Fund offers merely a financial deed. Respondents to the survey were questioned about the amount of money received and the procedure leading up to that.

The results show that while the Fund is entitled to grant victims up to 31.800 euro (22.700 to repair their economic losses (like lost income and medical expenses) and 9.100 for their non-economic losses (pain and suffering)), victims receive, on average 3.120 euro (1050 in economic compensation and 2070 euro for pain and suffering). Only 12% of the respondents indicated they had expected to receive much more compensation than they actually did. In contrast to the idea that victims want to receive as much money as possible, millions even, respondents to this survey had rather modest expectations, or even no expectations at all. Moreover, a large majority of recipients indicated to be satisfied with the amounts received.

In order to determine whether recipients' expressed level of satisfaction truly indicates how satisfied they were with the money awarded to them, an exploratory factor analysis was performed. Lerner (2003), after all, warns that that when people are asked to state how they feel about different aspects of an encounter with a specific authority, the answers to these different aspects may just reflect the respondents' attitude towards the authority in general (2003). Therefore, all variables which could potentially be part of a larger construct were included in the factor analysis. The results show there was indeed redundancy in the variables; they cluster onto two factors, which were labeled 'outcome satisfaction' and 'procedural satisfaction'.

---

72 A stepwise regression of all the variables associated with procedural satisfaction showed that the dummy variables 'did the procedure go quick or slow' and 'more or less than 2 times in contact with Fund', predicted procedural satisfaction the best; R equals .545, R^2=.297, $p<.001$, and the constant and beta's differed significantly from zero ($p<.001$).

As a result, recipients' satisfaction with compensation could not be considered without taking other outcome-related variables into account as well. The same goes for procedural variables like 'respectful treatment' and 'adequately informed during application': they turned out to be part of the general factor procedural satisfaction. Hence, the remainder of the analysis focused on 'outcome satisfaction' and 'procedural satisfaction'.

In order to determine why recipients of state compensation experience procedural satisfaction, several procedural aspects have been considered. The number of times recipient have been in contact with the Fund, for instance, and whether or not recipients filled in the application forms themselves, have been shown to positively correlate with procedural satisfaction. The same goes for how positive recipients are about the time lag between application and decision; those who regard the Fund's processing to be quick are significantly more satisfied about the procedure than are those who said the procedure was slow.

In other words, procedural aspects are important for procedural satisfaction. Financial aspects, on the other hand, are not. It does not matter how much compensation recipients received or how high that amount was compared to their disposable income. Surprisingly enough, these financial aspects did not affect recipients outcome satisfaction either. Apparently, the amount of money one receives is not that important to victims. How one receive compensation, however, does. Outcome satisfaction is significantly related to the amount of time it takes the Fund to decide on a case and more specifically, the qualification of that period; recipients who regard the process as 'quick' are particularly more satisfied about the outcome than are those who qualified the process as 'slow'.

In sum, no evidence was found to support the idea that financial aspects of compensation are of significant importance to recipients. Instead, recipients seem to be much more influenced by procedural matters. In light of the fact that the Dutch Crime Compensation Fund's sole purpose is to financially compensate victims, this finding is quite surprising. The results are in line, though, with the rich literature on procedural justice. After all, just like plaintiffs in a court case, recipients of state compensation seem to care more about *how* outcomes are reached, than about what that outcome actually is (Lind & Tyler, 1988; Tyler, 2006: p. 374).

Determining appropriate levels of compensation by means of the monetary value of pain and suffering, as suggested by Moore & Shepherd (2006, p. 293), is, therefore, difficult to defend from a victim's perspective. Such approaches, after all, strengthen the idea that all that matters is *how* the 'right' amount of compensation is assessed, while victims care much more about *how* one is compensated.

On the other hand, the results do not suggest financial implications are of no importance at all. It seems likely there is a threshold on the amount of money that is satisfying to victims. An award of 250 euro's for the pain and suffering of a rape victim, for instance, could well be considered insultingly low. Further research will be needed to determine which levels of compensation are perceived to be appropriate, and which are not.

References

Atkinson, G., Healey, A. & Mourato, S. (2005). Valuing the costs of violent crime: a stated preference approach. *Oxford Economic Papers*, 57 (4), pp. 559-585.

Cheon, A. & Regehr, C. (2006) Restorative justice models in cases of intimate partner violence: Revieweing the evidence. *Vicims & Offenders*, 1(4), pp. 369-94.

Cohen, M.A. (1988). Pain, suffering, and jury awards: a study of the cost of crime to victims. *Law and Society Review*, 22, pp. 537-555.

Cohen, M. A., Rust, R.T., Steen, S., Tidd, S.T. (2004). Willingness-to-Pay for crime control programs; *Criminology* 42(1): pp. 86-106.

Cooter, R. 2003. Hand rule damages for incompensable losses. *San Diego Law Review*, 40, pp. 1097-1121.

Croon, M.A. (2008), *Methods for correlational research: factor analysis, path analysis, and structural equation modeling*. Harlow: Pearson Custom Publishing.

Dolan, P., Loomes, G., Peasgood, T. & Tsuchiya, A. (2005), Estimating the intangible victims costs of violent crime. *Brit. J. Crimonology*, 45, p. 958-76.

Field, A.P. (2009). Discovering statistics using SPSS for Windows: Advanced techniques for the beginner (3th ed.). London: Sage

Frey, B.S., Benz, M. & Stutzer. A. (2004). Introducing procedural utility: not only what, but also how matters. *Journal of Institutional and Theoretical Economics*, 160(3), p. 377-401._

Groot, I., de Hoop, T., Houkes, A. & Sikkel, D. (2007). *De kosten van criminaliteit. Een onderzoek naar de kosten van criminaliteit voor tien verschillende delicttypen.* Amsterdam: SEO Economisch Onderzoek.

Kline, P. (1994). *An easy guide to factor analysis*. New York: Routledge.

Lerner, M.J. (2003). The justice motive: where social psychologists found it, how they lost it, and why they may not find it again. *Personality and Social Psychology Review*, 7 (4), pp. 388–399.

Lind, E.A. & Tyler, T.R. (1988), *The Social Psychology of Procedural Justice*. New York: Plenum Press.

Linting, M., Meulman, J.J., Groenen, P.J.F. & Van Der Kooij., A.J. (2007). Nonlinear principal components analysis: Introduction and application. *Psychological Methods*, 12(3), pp. 336–358.

Miller, T.R., Cohen, M.A. & Rossman, S.B. (1993) Victim costs of violent crime and resulting injuries. *Health Affairs*, 12(4), pp. 186-197.

Miller, T.R., Cohen, M.A., Wiersema, B. (1996). Victim Costs and Consequences: A New Look. National Institute of Justice/NCJRS, Rockville MD.

Moore, S. & Shepherd, J.P. (2006). The cost of fear: shadow pricing the intangible costs of crime. *Applied Economics*, 38(3), pp. 293-300.

Mulder, J.D.W.E. (2009a). How do we compensate a victim's losses? An Economic Perspective. *International Review of Victimology*, vol. 16, pp. 67–87.

Mulder, J.D.W.E. (2009b). *Compensatie na geweld. Wie krijgen er een vergoeding van het Schadefonds Geweldsmisdrijven en wat zijn de effecten van zo'n financiële vergoeding?* Tilburg: Intervict/PrismaPrint.

Mulder, J.D.W.E. (2010), Hoe schadevergoeding kan leiden tot gevoelens van erkenning en gerechtigheid. Lessen uit de praktijk van het Schadefonds Geweldsmisdrijven. *Nederlands Juristenblad*, jrg. 85, pp. 293-296.

O'Connell, M. (2003). *Criminal Injuries Compensation. Revisiting the rationale for state funded compensation for crime victims.* Paper presented at the Innovation: Promising Practices for Victims and Witnesses in the Criminal Justice System – A National Conference, Canberra, 23 – 24 June, 2003.

Okimoto, T. G., & Tyler, T.R. (2007), Is compensation enough? Relational concerns in responding to unintended inequity. *Group Processes & Intergroup Relations*, 10(3), pp. 399-420.

Pemberton, A. (2010), Needs of victims of terrorism. In Letschert, R.M., Staiger, I., & Pemberton, A. (eds.). *Assisting victims of terrorism: Towards a European standard of justice*. Dordrecht: Springer.

Strang, H. (2002), *Repair or revenge: victims and restorative justice*. Oxford: Oxford University Press.

Sunstein, C. R. (2008). Illusory Losses, Journal of Legal Studies, 37(2), pp. 157-194.

Tyler, T.R. (2006). Process utility and help seeking: what do people want from experts? *Journal of Economic Psychology*, 27, pp. 360–376.

Appendix A: statistical analysis

Exploratory factor analysis

Exploratory factor analysis (EFA) seeks to uncover the underlying structure of a relatively large set of variables. The researcher's *à priori* assumption is that any indicator may be associated with any factor. This is the most common form of factor analysis. There is no prior theory and one uses factor loadings to intuit the factor structure of the data.

EFA are performed by examining the pattern of correlations (or covariances) between the observed measures. Variables that are highly correlated (either positively or negatively) are likely influenced by the same factors, while those that are relatively uncorrelated are likely influenced by different factors. There are several different types of factor analysis, with the most common being *principal components analysis* (PCA), which is preferred for purposes of data reduction, as I do in this paper.[73]

Factor analysis is part of the general linear model (GLM) family of procedures, and as a consequence, only variables scaled at the continuous level (interval or ratio level of measurement) may be analyzed by means of EFA (see Field, 2009, p. 133 and 631-3). If data is based on Likert scales, like in this study, variables are considered to be scaled ordinal instead of continuously. Hence, if one wishes to explore whether variables could be reduced to a smaller number, one can either simply presume variables to be linear (as one often does, see Field, 2009, p. 650), or transform the variables by means of categorical principal component analysis (CATPCA). I choose to do the latter.

Transformation of variables

CATPCA is a non-trivial function of SPSS which commences analysis via optimal quantification (also referred to as optimal scaling, or optimal scoring) a process whereby categories of the categorical variables are appointed continuous numeric values (Linting, 2007, p. 13). This process provides the numeric values that are required for variance and Pearson correlation calculations (Linting, 2007, p. 12-3). Like traditional principal component analysis (PCA), CATPCA attempts to extract factors that can account for as much variance in the variables as possible. In other words, it is possible with CATPA to perform a 'normal' factor analysis with non-linear data.

I, however, choose to extract the transformed data by means of traditional PCA. Reason for doing so, is that PCA offers the possibility to rotate factors, which simplifies the factor structure and therefore makes its interpretation

---

73 Although factor analysis and principal component analysis are strictly speaking two different techniques, the terms are commonly used interchangeably, as I will do here too (see Field, 2009, p. 638). Moreover, the two procedures often yield similar results (see Field, 2009, p. 638, 651).

easier and more reliable (Pedhazur & Schmelkin, 1991, p. 611).

Principal component analysis (PCA) with varimax rotation and Kaiser normalisation.
There are several ways to rotate extracted factors (see Field, 2009, p. 644). The exact choice of rotation depends largely on whether the underlying factors are, or should be, related. Orthogonal rotation is used for independent factors (whereby the varimax method is recommended) and if factors are supposed to correlate, direct oblimin rotation should be selected (Field, 2009, p. 644). If there are no theoretical grounds to suspect relatedness, one may choose to start with the direct oblimin rotation, and if it turns out the extracted factors are not related, to run a subsequent analysis with orthogonal rotation.

Seeing that there are no theoretical grounds for either suspecting relatedness, nor unrelatedness of factors in the present study, I choose to start with the direct oblimin rotation. The results showed that extracted components may be interpreted as independent (r_s=-0,082, ns), hence I proceeded the analysis by means of the orthogonal varimax rotation.

Extraction of factors
In order to ascertain if and how, the survey variables were driven by an underlying variable like general satisfaction with the Fund, the following 10 variables were included in the analysis;

1. 'Knowledge of application process', related survey question: Was it clear to you how the Crime Compensation Fund would determine whether you were eligible for compensation? (5 possible answers ranging from 'Not at all' to 'To a great extent')
2. 'Respectful treatment', related survey question: Have you always been treated with respect by the Crime Compensation Fund? (7 possible answers ranging from 'Most definitely not' to 'Most certainly')
3. 'Adequately informed during application', related survey question: Do you think the Crime Compensation Fund kept you well enough informed about the handling of your case? (5 possible answers ranging from 'Not at all' to 'To a great extent')
4. 'Fair handling of cases' related survey question: How fair do you think the Crime Compensation Fund handled your case? (5 possible answers ranging from 'Highly unfair' to 'Highly fair')
5. 'Specific circumstances taken into account', related survey question: Do you think the Crime Compensation Fund sufficiently reviewed the specific circumstances of your case? (5 possible answers ranging from 'Not at all' to 'To a great extent')
6. 'Satisfaction with total amount of compensation', related survey question: How satisfied were you with the total amount of money that you received from the Crime Compensation Fund? (7 possible answers ranging from 'Very unsatisfied' to 'Very satisfied')

7. 'Compensation matched expectations', related survey question: Did the compensation you received match the expectations you had? (5 possible answers ranging from 'I expected to receive a lot more' to 'I expected a lot less')
8. 'Satisfaction with award for pain and suffering', related survey question: How satisfied were you with the compensation for pain and suffering? (7 possible answers ranging from 'Very unsatisfied' to 'Very satisfied')
9. 'Unnecesarry questions', related survey question: Do you think there were unnecessary questions you had to answer on the application form (3 possible answers ranging from 'Not at all' to 'Yes, many questions appeared redundant to me'
10. 'Processing time', related survey question: What did you think about the time you had the wait for Fund's decision? (5 answer possibilities ranging from 'Very slow' to 'Very quick')

Based on these ten variables PCA extracted three factors with eigenvalues over Kaiser's criterion of 1. This criterion is based on the idea that eigenvalues represent the amount of variation explained by a factor, and that a eigenvalue of 1 represents a substantial amount of variation.

Yet, another tool to decide how many factors should be extracted, the scree plot, justified retaining just 2 components. In a scree plot, each eigenvalue is plotted against the factor with which it is associated with. The curve's point of inflexion, is said to be the cut-off point for selecting factors (see Field, 2009). In our case that meant retaining just 2 factors.

As the variables 'unnecesarry questions' and 'processing time' scored rather poorly on the KMO statistic (see below), (respectively .193 and.218 instead of the bare minimum of .5), I excluded them from the analysis (as recommended by Field, 2009, p. 659). The eight remaining variables clustered onto two factors (see Table A1), both confirmed by Kaiser's criterion and the scree plot.

Table A.1: Results of the orthogonal exploratory factor analysis (N=217)

	Component	
	1	2
1 Knowledge of application process		0,738
2 Respectful treatment		0,705
3 Adequately informed		0,601
4 Fair handling of cases	0,772	
5 Specific circumstances taken into account	0,780	
6 Satisfaction with total amount of compensation	0,854	
7 Compensation matched expectations	0,810	
8 Satisfaction with award for pain and suffering	0,632	

The factor loadings as shown in Table A1 are the correlation coefficients between the variables (rows) and factors (columns). Analogous to Pearson's r, the squared factor loading is the percent of variance in that indicator variable explained by the factor. Here, the two components explain 61% of the variables' variance.

I have to note, however, that due to the relatively small sample size (<250), only factors that load more than 0.450 are reported (as recommended by Field, 2009).

Reliability of the analysis

The reliability of factor analysis depends, among others, on the sample size. Tabachnick & Fidell (2007), for instance, agree that it is comforting to have at least 300 cases for factor analysis. Others, however, claim that less than 100 may be perfectly adequate (see Field, 2009, p. 647). In order to study the adequacy of the present sample, I used the Kaiser-Meyer-Olkin measure of sampling adequacy (KMO). This statistic varies between 0 and 1. A value of 0 indicates diffusion in the pattern of correlation. Hence, factor analysis is likely to be inappropriate. A value close to 1, on the other hand, indicates the patterns of correlations are relatively compact and so factor analysis should yield distinct and reliable factors. According to Field (2009, p. 647) KMO values between 0.7 and 0.8 are good and values between 0.8 and 0.9 great. The KMO of 0.797 of the present study, therefore, is considered to be a good or even great result. As KMO values for the individual items were al >0.606, which is well above the individual minimum of .500, it seems valid to say our sample of 217 respondents yields distinct and reliable factors.

Reliability of the factor analysis also relies on the intercorrelation between variables. There are essentially two potential problems: 1) correlations that are not high enough, and 2) correlations that are too high. Bartlett's test of sphericity can be used to test whether correlations are high enough, while the determinant of the correlation matrix indicates whether correlations are low enough. In the present study, Bartlett's test indicated that correlations between items were sufficiently large, as the test turned out to be highly significant (chi-square (28)= 626,906, p<0.01). The determinant of the correlation matrix, on the other hand, equaled .024, which is much bigger than the limit of .00001. Hence, multicollinearity is not a problem in our analysis.

Reliability of the factors themselves, can be expressed by means of Crombach's alpha. According to the CATPCA analysis, Crombach's alpha equals .908 for our analysis, so we can assume the overall reliability of the items is good (alpha>0.8 are good according to Field, p. 681).

Factor labels

As statistics programs do not assign labels to the factors it distracts, interpretation of the factors' labels is left up to the researcher's discretion.

There are a few rules suggested by methodologists: factor names should

- be brief, one or two words
- communicate the nature of the underlying construct

How does one come up with an appropriate label? First of all, variables with the highest loadings are considered the most important (Croon, 2006; Kline 1994). Therefore, these variables should influence the label selected for each factor to a great extent (Croon, 2006, p. 67). Secondly, one may look for patterns of similarity between items that load on a factor. If seeking to validate a theoretical structure, one could use the factor names that already exist in the literature. Otherwise, one should use names that will communicate the conceptual structure to others. In addition, one can look at the items that do not load on a factor, to determine what that factor isn't. All and all, choosing an appropriate it is a rather subjective process.

As explained in the paper, the factors extracted in the present study, could be interpreted fairly easy. After all, the factor analysis showed a clear distinction between outcome and procedure related variables (see Table A1).

References

Croon, M.A. (2008), *Methods for correlational research: factor analysis, path analysis, and structural equation modeling*. Harlow: Pearson Custom Publishing.

Field, A.P. (2009). Discovering statistics using SPSS for Windows: Advanced techniques for the beginner (3th ed.). London: Sage

Kline, P. (1994). *An easy guide to factor analysis.* New York: Routledge.

Linting, M. (2007), *Nonparametric inference in nonlinear principal components analysis: exploration and beyond.* Doctoral Thesis, Leiden University, the Netherlands.

Pedhazur, E. J., & Schmelkin, L. P. (1991). *Measurement, design, and analysis: An integrated approach.* Hillsdale, NJ: Erlbaum.

Tabachnick, B. G., and Fidell, L. S. (2007). *Using Multivariate Statistics, 5th ed.* Boston: Allyn and Bacon.

The symbolic value of financial compensation

An empirical analysis of how victims perceive compensation

By J.D.W.E. Mulder

Introduction

Why do victims of personal injury want to receive financial compensation for their losses? Is it to acquire a fair amount of money for the wrong they have endured, or do they have other, more symbolic reasons to file for compensation? Many economists will probably presume the first. Economic analysis has, after all, focused on instrumental outcomes since the 1930's (see Frey, Benz & Stutzer, 2004). As a result one tends to define people's preferences over actual, monetary, outcomes (see for example Viscusi, 1996; Calfee & Rubin, 1992).

Scholars from other disciplines, however, stress the symbolic value of compensation. One assumes, for example, that financial compensation is perceived by victims as an acknowledgement of their victimization, and as an affirmation of their innocence (see Cobley, 1998). Moreover, if financial reparations are made by the state, compensation is said to reinforce the bonds that bind people together (Dignan, 2005, p. 44).

Surprisingly little is known about how recipients of financial compensation perceive the money awarded to them. Up till now, very few studies have considered their perspective. Relis (2007) interviewed claimants in medical malpractice cases and shows that they do not go to court for 'the money'. Instead they have objectives like obtaining admissions of fault, prevention of recurrences, retribution, answers, apologies and acknowledgements of harm (Relis, 2007).

These results suggests that victims primarily have symbolic reasons to go to court and no apparent financial ones. But why do they claim financial reparation then? Perhaps feelings of acknowledgement and respect occur *because* one receives monetary compensation, as argued by Feldthuysen et al. (2000)?

In order to learn how financial compensation affects recipients, and why victims apply for reparation in the first place, I conducted an explorative study among victims of personal injury. More in particular, I conducted a survey among 217 victims of violent crime who received compensation from the Dutch Crime Compensation Fund. This state-run fund offers financial reparation to all victims of violent crime who have not been fully compensated through other means. Due to its focus on financial matters, I was interested to learn whether victims apply with the Fund out of mere financial motives, or if symbolic objectives are of importance too.

Moreover, I was interested to learn what financial compensation means to those receiving it. Do victims attribute symbolic values like acknowledgement and affirmation of their innocence to compensation? And if so, why? Does the Dutch state's involvement matter, for instance?

This paper offers the answers to these questions. It shows, for instance, that one in four victims filed a claim in order to receive acknowledgement and finding closure.[74] Moreover, a majority of respondents agreed with symbolic statements like 'The financial award of the Crime Compensation Fund was a form of emotional support to me' (75%), and 'Receiving an award from the Crime Compensation Fund helped me to cope with the aftermath of the crime'(56%). No less than 83% found the award to be an acknowledgement of their victimization.

Most of these symbolic values are described as separate, independent variables, within the literature. Yet, they turn out to be closely related to one another. The seven variables explored in this study cluster onto two general constructs. The first one contains all variables that are more or less internally focused (like acknowledgement and coping with the aftermath of crime), while the other one exists of values that involve others and is thus more outward focused.

Statistical analysis shows that how respondents scored on both constructs is not affected by one's gender or age, or the type of crime one endured. Nor was the amount of compensation of any influence. What did affect one's score was whether or not one has knowledge about the state's involvement with the Crime Compensation Fund. Those who knew the Fund is publicly financed, attribute significantly more internal and external symbolic value to the money they received, than do those who did not knew the state was involved. This result confirms the proposition that involvement of the state is of importance to victims.

All in all, this paper is one of the first to provide information on how victims themselves perceive the compensation awarded to them. It is organized as follows. Section 1 presents the study's design. Results are presented in section 2, and section 3 provides a short discussion.

---

74 Respondents were asked to describe the main reason for their application with the fund. They were asked to do so in their own words, no possible answers were given.

1. Methodology

1.1. Dutch Crime Compensation Fund

From the 1960's onwards, crime compensation funds were founded all over the globe (O'Connell, 2003).[75] These state run funds offer financial reparation to victims of violent crime who are not able to obtain financial compensation elsewhere. The Dutch Crime Compensation Fund (hereafter the Fund) is one of those funds. It was established in 1976 and is part of the Dutch Ministry of Justice.[76]

The Dutch Crime Compensation Fund awards financial compensation to persons victimized by crimes of violence. Hence, victims of crimes like attempted homicide, rape, stalking and domestic violence, may file a claim with the Fund. One can do so by means of a written application form. If the Fund approves one's application, the victim will be awarded either economic compensation to repair its economic losses (like medical expenses and lost income), non-economic compensation to cover pain and suffering, or both. The amount of economic compensation that the Fund awards, depends on the costs incurred – up to a maximum of 22.700 euro. Compensation for pain and suffering is determined by use of 8 scales, ranging from 550 to 9.100 euro.[77]

Noteworthy is that during its proceedings, the Fund does not show any relational concern. For example, the Fund does not try to appease the victim, or specifically acknowledge the harm that has been caused (e.g. Okimoto & Tyler, 2007). Nor does the Fund endorse the government's involvement.[78] In essence, all the Dutch Crime Compensation Fund does, is offering financial reparation for the losses that victims of violence incur.

---

75 New Zealand was the first to found a crime compensation fund in 1963, Britain followed in 1964, and California and Wisconsin in 1965. Nowadays state compensation schemes operate in many countries, including Austria, Australia, Belgium, Bermuda, Canada, Columbia, Denmark, Germany, Finland, France, Hong Kong, Ireland, Israel, Italy, Japan, Luxembourg, the Netherlands, Northern Ireland, Norway, Philippines, Poland, Portugal, Scotland, Spain, Sweden, Switzerland, and United Arab Emirates (O'Connell, 2003).

76 The fund is financed through general tax revenues. For more information about the fund see: www.schadefonds.nl/en_GB/algemeen/

77 A standardized list of physical injuries plus an evaluation of the nature, circumstances, and consequences of the crime determines the level of non-economic compensation that the Fund awards (see Schadefonds Geweldsmisdrijven, 2007).

78 The offender is not involved either. In some countries, convicted offenders are obliged to contribute to the compensation Fund. In the Netherlands, this is not the case. All is paid for by general tax revenues

1.2. *The study*

The current study is part of a larger study into the effects of financial compensation (see Mulder, 2009a, 2009b, 2010). Participants were recruited through the Dutch Crime Compensation Fund in the spring of 2009. In total, 1000 victims were approached to fill out a survey concerning the financial compensation they had received in 2008.[79] 217 recipients returned a copy that was usable for analysis (out of 225). Furthermore, the Fund provided additional information from their files.

In order to explore the symbolic value of financial reparation, the survey covered the following topics:

Motives for application. The Dutch Crime Compensation Fund offers victims financial reparation for their losses, nothing more nothing less. As a result, it seems apparent that victims' main or even sole reason for applying with the fund is to obtain compensation. Yet, according to Feldthusen et al. (2000, p. 75) victims perceive a claiming process as having a role in the recovery of their well-being; victims would enter a process of compensation with explicit therapeutic expectations. These conflicting views raise the question why victims file for financial compensation with a Crime Compensation Fund. Do they apply out of symbolic motives? Or financial ones? Or perhaps both? In order to find an answer to these questions, respondents to the survey were asked to tell in their own words why they had filed a claim with the Fund.

State's involvement. Many scholars have argued that due to the state's involvement money granted by crime compensation funds has symbolic meaning to recipients. State compensation would, for instance, 'serve symbolically to reforge the bonds that bind people together'(Dignan, 2005, p. 44). Subsequently, state compensation would give victims a sense of empowerment, validation and integration into the social order (Young, 2003). Freckelton (2004) even speaks of a "therapeutically symbolic gesture of collegiality and concern" (p. 58-9). Yet, up till now there is no empirical evidence that either proves or contradicts these statements. So in attempt to ascertain whether the state's involvement affects the symbolic value of compensation, respondents to the survey were asked to indicate whether they were aware of the Dutch state's involvement with the fund or not.

Symbolic value. As said, many scholars have argued that compensation has symbolic value. Cobley (1998), for instance, purports that financial compensation is perceived by victims as an acknowledgement of their victimization, and as an affirmation of their innocence (see Cobley, 1998). In order to explore whether recipients of compensation indeed agree, the

[79] In 2008 a total of 4459 victims was granted compensation by the Dutch Crime Compensation Fund.

survey included the following seven statements.

1. The award of the Crime Compensation Fund reduced my pain and suffering
2. The award of the Crime Compensation Fund made me feel acknowledged as a victim
3. The award of the Crime Compensation Fund was a form of emotional support to me
4. Receiving an award from the Crime Compensation Fund confirmed my innocence
5. The award of the Crime Compensation Fund was a form of justice to me
6. Receiving an award from the Crime Compensation Fund helped me to cope with the aftermath of the crime.
7. Victims of crimes of violence are entitled to financial compensation.

These statements are a reflection of the diverse definitions of symbolic value that scholars have used so far, and they also coincide with the theory of therapeutic jurisprudence. This theory is recognized as an important model for assessing the impact that various aspects of the legal system has on its participants (Wexler & Wininck, 1996). Maercker & Muller (2004), for instance have shown how social acknowledgement is important to victims; their recovery is connected to positive social reactions which show appreciation for the unique state the victim is in, and which acknowledge the victim's current difficult situation. Other important therapeutic factors are: coping with the emotional consequences of crime (Feldthusen et al., 2000, p. 69), the need to see justice done (Orth, 2003), and a reduction of self-blame (Janoff-Bulman, 1985). All these therapeutic factors were reflected in the survey statements.

1.3. The sample

All 217 recipients of state compensation who responded to the survey have been victims of violent crime. One in four, for example, was victim of a (severe) sexual crime and one in ten of severe physical abuse. Table 1 provides an overview.

Table 1: Types of crime suffered by respondents (N=217)

Type of crime	percentage of respondents*
Homicide and manslaughter	1
Attempted homicide and manslaughter	7
Severe sexual crimes**	15
Sexual crimes***	9
Violent theft	24
Assault and battery	24
Severe assault ***	11
Threat*****	7

* Because of rounding, the total does not add up to 100
** among others: rape, involuntarily prostitution, intercourse with someone under the age of 12
*** among others: fornication, (attempted) sexual violation
**** among others: hostage taking, kidnapping and severe physical abuse
***** among others: extortion, stalking

Table 2: Compensation awarded to respondents in euro's (N=217)

	Economic compensation	Non-economic compensation	Total compensation
Mean	1053	2071	3124
Median	161	2100	2750
Mode	0	550	550
Std. Deviation	2529	1471	3064
Minimum	0	0*	90
Maximum	21317	8250	23417
Skewness	5	1	3

* Due to the fact that relatives of murdered victims are not entitled to non-economic compensation under Dutch law, the minimum award for pain and suffering equals zero.

Approximately half of the respondents was female (52%). Average age at the time of application was 38 years (range 0-88, sd=19).[80] Respondents' income of respondents was relatively low: 65% had a disposable income of less than 20.000 euro a year.[81] On average respondents received 3100 euro

80 Most respondents were between the age of 15 and 25 (29%), which is in line with the fact that young people run the highest risk of falling victim to crime (see Mulder, 2009b, p. 9).

81 36% of the respondents indicated to have a disposable income of less than 10.000 euro a year, which is rather low compared to the fact that only 5% of all Dutch citizens has less

from the Dutch Crime Compensation Fund: 2070 euro for pain and suffering and 930 euro to cover economic losses. Yet, as table 2 shows, amounts varied considerably.

1.3.1. *Non-response*

Whilst the sample of respondents cannot be taken as representative of all the Fund's recipients as a whole, there is no reason to believe it is atypical. A comparison of the sample (N=217) with the total group of recipients approached for participation (N=1000), shows resemblance on aspects like gender, age, type of crime and compensation (see table 3).

Table 3: Comparison of respondents to survey (N=217) and recipients approached for participation (N=1000).

	Gender	Average age	Percentage severe crime*	Percentage less severe crime*	length of procedure (in days)	Average amount non-economic compensation	Average amount total compensation
Respondents to survey	52% female	38 (SD=19)	35%	65%	89 (sd=53)	2140 euro (sd=1445)	3120 euro (sd= 3064)
Recipients approached	53% female	36 (SD=17)	32%	68%	92 (sd=56)	2130 euro (sd=1500)	3080 euro (sd=2800)

* The category 'severe crime' consists of homicide & manslaughter, attempted homicide & manslaughter, severe sexual crimes and severe assault. Less severe crimes are sexual crimes, violent theft, assault and battery and threat.

2. Results

2.1. *Victims' reasons to apply for compensation*

In order to learn why victims would like to receive financial compensation for their losses, respondents to the survey were asked to explain in their own words why they had filled a claim. Some recipients were able to answer this question in just a few words, others used up to half a page. Nevertheless, three general motives for application could be distinguished (See Table 4).

First of all, most respondents described a financial motive for their application. They indicated, for example, that money was sought to cover legal costs, moving expenses, or just as a matter of principle. Secondly, a significant number of respondents mentioned symbolic motives; one in four described acknowledgement, atonement or finding closure as their main reason to submit an application. Thirdly, one in twelve filed a claim because they were

than 10.000 euro to spend annually. Moreover, 29% of the respondents indicated to have an income of 10-20.000 euro, while only 25% of the Dutch population has such an income.

(strongly) advised to do so by Victim Support Netherlands, the police, or their lawyer.

Table 4: Reasons victims have for submitting a claim with the Crime Compensation Fund (N=217)

	percentage of respondents
Financial motives	44%
Symbolic motives	26%
Advized by others	8%
Other	6%
Do not know	15%

Noteworthy is that no apparent differences in recipients' motives to file for state compensation could be found. For example, not more women than men described symbolic reasons, nor were there significant differences between victims of severe and less severe crimes (see Appendix 1).

2.2. *Knowledge about state's involvement*

Are recipients of state compensation aware of the fact they received public money? According to the survey results a majority of respondents is (64%). Just over one in three is not (see Table 4).

Table 5: Are recipients aware of the fact that the Fund awards victims public money? (N=217)

Knowledge about Fund's public function	Percentage of cases
No, I did not know the fund provided public money	36
Yes, I was aware of the fact that the fund provides public money	64
Total	100%

Here too, no differences could be found between groups of respondents. Not more men than women knew about the state's involvement, for instance. Nor are those who applied out of symbolic objectives more familiar with the state's involvement than those who had other objectives (see Appendix 2).

2.3. *Symbolic affect*

Compensation and state compensation in particular is said to affect recipients in a non-financial, symbolic way (see Freckelton, 2004; Feldthusen et al. 2000). In order explore how recipients themselves think about the effects of compensation, respondents to the survey were asked to indicate on a 7-point scale whether they agreed with the following statements;

- Receiving a financial award from the Crime Compensation Fund supported me emotionally
- Receiving a financial award from the Crime Compensation Fund was a form of justice to me
- The financial award of the Crime Compensation Fund made me feel acknowledged as a victim
- The financial award of the Crime Compensation Fund reduced my pain and suffering
- Receiving a financial award from the Crime Compensation Fund helped me to cope with the aftermath of the crime.
- Receiving a financial award from the Crime Compensation Fund confirmed my innocence
- Victims of crimes of violence are entitled to financial compensation.

As Table 5 shows; a majority of respondents agreed with all statements. A large majority (83%), for instance, believed the award to be an acknowledgement of their victimization, and eight out of ten victims find the award to be a form of justice (see Table 5). Moreover, three out of four respondents (75%) agreed with the statement: 'I found the award of the Compensation Fund to be a form of emotional support', and 61% even thinks the award reduced their pain and suffering. A further 85% believes that victims are entitled to financial compensation, and over half (54%) found the award to confirm their own innocence (see table 5).

Table 6: Does state compensation have symbolic value according to those receiving it (N=217)?

	Emotional support	Form of justice to me	Acknow-ledgement as a victim	Reduction of pain and suffering	Coping aftermath of the crime	Confir-mation of innocence	Entitle-ment
Strongly disagree	2	1	1	5	7	4	0
Disagree	6	2	4	13	13	8	1
Slightly disagree	5	3	1	5	5	4	2
Neutral	12	11	10	13	15	23	12
Slightly agree	20	16	13	30	25	9	10
Agree	38	38	46	24	22	28	43
Stronly agree	17	26	23	7	9	17	29
Don't know	2	3	2	2	4	7	3
Total	100%	100%	100%	100%	100%	100%	100%

In other words, a (large) majority of the respondents agreed with the distinguished statements. Hence, according to victims themselves, compensation granted by the Dutch Crime Compensation Fund indeed provides symbolic value to recipients.

Often one describes values like acknowledgement and confirmation of innocence as separate, independent, variables. But are they? According to Table 5 respondents agree more strongly with some statements than with others. Is there a pattern? Well, according to correlation analysis there is: all seven variables are significantly related to one another (see Table 6).[82] Hence, is seems invalid to qualify the symbolic variables as separate and independent. How they should be interpreted instead, will be explored in the upcoming paragraph.

Table 7: Spearman's correlations of symbolic variables

	1	2	3	4	5	6	7
1 Reduction of pain and suffering	1,000						
2 Acknowledgement as a victim	,406**	1,000					
3 Emotional support	,425**	,602**	1,000				
4 Confirmation of innocence	,206**	,375**	,285**	1,000			
5 Form of justice to me	,208**	,373**	,319**	,345**	1,000		
6 Coping with aftermath of the crime	,565**	,355**	,416**	,221**	,211**	1,000	
7 Entitlement	,016	,212**	,078	,298**	,420**	,106	1,000

** Correlation is significant at 0.01 level (2-sided)

2.3.1. *Interrelatedness of symbolic variables*

A widely used statistics tool which helps to detect possible structures in the relationships between variables is exploratory factor analysis (Kline, 1994). This statistical program examines which variables cluster together in a meaningful way: it looks for variables that correlate highly with a group of other variables, but do not correlate with variables outside that group. In order to use this statistic tool, all variables have to be of a linear nature. As our variables were based on a 7-point Likert scale, which cannot be assumed

82 Since the observed variables are measured on a Likert scale, which cannot be assumed to be linear, one could question the use of a correlation analysis. I nevertheless choose to report these results as no immediate conclusions are drawn from them, while they do provide a valuable indication of variable interrelatedness.

to be linear, the variables were transformed through categorical principal component analysis (CATPCA) (see Linting et al., 2007). Subsequently, an orthogonal exploratory factor analysis was performed. Table 7 shows the results.[83]

Table 8: Factor loadings based on a principle components analysis with varimax rotation for 7 items (N = 217)

	Component	
	1	2
Victims are entitled to such an award	,763	
Receiving a financial award was a form of justice to me	,786	
Receiving a financial award was a confirmation of my innocence	,684	
Receiving a financial award helped me cope with the aftermath of the crime		,794
The financial award has given me acknowledgement as a victim		,643
Receiving a financial award supported me emotionally		,757
The financial award has eased my pain & suffering		,826

As shown in Table 7, the symbolic variables cluster onto two factors. Hence, there is redundancy in the variables. Apparent is how all variables load highly onto the factors; correlations between the variables and factors range from .643 till .826.[84] This implies that the factors explain 41% up to 68% of the variance in the variables, which is considered a good result (Croon, 2006). Together the components account for a significant proportion (62%) of the variance in the transformed variables.

---

[83] A orthogonal rotation was chosen to report, as the oblimin rotation showed that both components can be seen as independent (component correlation matrix reports values of 1 and 0,219). Furthermore, only factors that load more than 0.5 are shown. The Kaiser-Meyer-Olkin measure verified sampling adequacy for the analysis, KMO=0.739 (good according to Field, 2009) and all KMO values for individual items were >0.605, which is well above the acceptable limit of 0.5. Bartlett's test of sphericity (chi square (21)= 395,961, $p<0.000$), indicated that correlations between items were sufficiently large for PCA. The diagonals of the anti-image correlation matrix were all over .5, supporting the inclusion of each item in the factor analysis. An initial analysis was run to obtain eigenvalues for each component in the data. Two components had eigenvalues over Kaiser's criterion of 1 and in combination explained 62% of the variance. The scree plot's inflexions justified retaining two components. Furthermore, CATPCA shows that crombach's alpha for both components equals .896, so we can assume that the overall reliability of the items is good (see Field, p. 681).

[84] Loadings of +- .5 or greater are considered practically significant, loadings exceeding .7 are considered indicative of well-defined structure. Moreover, loading of .8 and above are viewed as extremely high (Croon, 2006, p. 64).

The fact that all variables load highly onto the factors, tells us that the variables do not reflect seven separate elements of symbolic value. Instead, they provide information about two general constructs. Interpretation of these general constructs largely depends on the variables with the highest factor loadings, as these are considered to be the most important (Croon, 2006; Kline 1994).[85] Hence, the variables 'receiving a financial award was a form of justice to me' and 'the financial award has eased my pain & suffering' influence the two factors to a great extent (Croon, 2006, p. 67), which should be reflected in the factor's label.

How to choose an appropriate label? Looking at the two most important statements, it appears that symbolic value has a social, or external, component and a more personal, or internal, one. This distinction becomes even more apparent if we take the variables that load onto both factors too into account as well. After all, entitlement, a form of justice and confirmation of one's innocence (factor 1), do not only consider the victim's personal circumstances; they involve the victim's social standing. The variables that load onto factor 2 on the other hand, only concern the victim itself. Therefore, 'external symbolic value' seems an appropriate label for factor 1 and 'internal symbolic value' for factor 2.

In sum, a majority of the recipients agreed with the statements concerning symbolic value. Yet, the seven statements do not reflect separate elements of symbolic value. Exploratory factor analysis clearly shows that two general constructs underlie the seven variables. As a result it is not valid to analyze the seven statement variables independently. Instead, symbolic value should be addressed by means of 'external symbolic value' and 'internal symbolic value'.

2.3.2. *What affects the symbolic value of compensation?*

We have seen how victims attribute symbolic value to the compensation they receive. But why do they? Has it to do with that respondents received public money, as argued by many authors? Or is it simply the amount of money that affects the level of symbolic value?

Let's start with the recipient's knowledge about the fund's public funding. Do victims who are aware of the state's involvement with the crime compensation fund, score significantly higher on the two symbolic factors than do victims who did not know they received public money? Well, indeed they do ($U=4619$, $z=-4{,}868$, $p<0.05$, $r=.33$ in case of internal symbolic value

---

[85] Statistics programs do not assign labels to the factors it distracts during factor analysis. Therefore, interpretation of the factors' labels is left up to the researcher's discretion (Croon, 2006; Kline, 1994).

and U=4667, z=-4,763, p<0.05, r=.32 with regards to external symbolic value). Regression analysis confirms these results; 10% of the variance in scores on the two symbolic factors can be explained with the knowledge one has about the state's involvement.[86] Hence, there seems indeed to be truth in the statements of authors who argue that state compensation has symbolic value to recipients.

The amount of money one received, on the other hand, seems of no importance (see table 8). Recipients who received 5000 euro do not score significantly higher or lower on the two symbolic factors than do those who received 500 euro. Nor do the factor scores correlate with the victim's yearly income or, for that matter, with the ratio of one's award and yearly disposable income. In other words, the financial consequences of compensation do not affect the symbolic value attributed to the award received.

Table 9: Two-sided Spearman's correlation analysis of scores on factor 1 and compensation (N=183)

	1	2	3	4	5	6	7
1 Factor 1_external symbolic value	1,000						
2 Factor 2_internal symbolic value	0,03	1,000					
3 Compensation for pain and suffering	-,032	-,034	1,000				
4 Total amount of compensation	-,003	-,007	,785**	1,000			
5 Yearly disposable income	-,066	,131	-,054	-,022	1,000		
6 Total compensation/yearly disposable income	-,048	-,050	,617**	,742**	-,652**	1,000	
7 Compensation for pain and suffering/ yearly disposable income	-,052	-,040	,743**	,535**	-,676**	,860**	1,000

** correlation is significant at .01 level

Other explaining variables for why victims experience symbolic value could not be determined. There are no differences between males and females (internal symbolic value U=5850, z=-.065, ns; external symbolic value:

[86] Predicting symbolic value by means of one's knowledge about the state's involvement, resulted in a model in which R equals .325, R^2=.11, p<.001. Both the constant and beta differed significantly from zero (p<.001).

U=5550, z=-.053; ns), types of crimes (internal symbolic value: H(7)=11.283, ns; external symbolic value: H(7)=5.479, ns), ages groups (internal symbolic value: H(6)=3.661, ns; external symbolic value: H(6)=2.596, ns) and income groups (internal symbolic value: H(4)=3.641, ns; external symbolic value: H(4)=6.036, ns) with respect to the scores on the two symbolic factors. It does not even matter whether respondents described symbolic motives for filling a claim or not (internal symbolic value: H=3.482, ns; external symbolic value: H=6.883, ns).

3. Discussion & conclusion

This paper explores the symbolic value of state compensation. According to several scholars this type of compensation entails more to recipients than a mere financial deed. It, for example, would mend the bonds that bind people together (Dignan, 2005, p. 44), give victims a sense of empowerment, validation and integration into the social order (Young, 2003) and serve as a 'therapeutically symbolic gesture of collegiality and concern' (Freckelton, 2004, p. 58-9).

In order to explore whether state compensation truly entails more to victims of crime, this paper expounds the results of a survey held among 217 victims of violent crime who received financial compensation from the Dutch Crime Compensation Fund. The results show that one in four respondents had symbolic motives for filling a claim. They, for instance, hoped to be acknowledged as a victim and to find closure. This is in line with Feldthusen et al. (2000) who states that victims expect a claiming process to have a role in the recovery of their emotional well-being.

But does receiving money actually live up to such expectations? Do recipients feel acknowledged as a victim for example? Well, seeing that 83% of the respondents agreed with the statement "The financial award of the Crime Compensation Fund made me feel acknowledged as a victim", it seems it does. Moreover, three out of four respondents (75%) agreed with the statement: 'I found the award of the Compensation Fund to be a form of emotional support', and a further 54% found the award to confirm their innocence.

In other words, the survey results show that recipients of state compensation contribute symbolic value to the money they received. However, further analysis of these results shows that instead of various independent types of symbolic value, there are two general constructs that underlie the explored symbolic variables, namely internal and external symbolic value. As a result, it is not valid to conclude that state compensation acknowledges recipients as victims or that state compensation helps victims to cope with the aftermath of the crime, for that matter. Instead, we may conclude that state compensation offers recipients a general sense of 'internal symbolic value'.

In a similar way, we cannot purport that state compensation offers recipients a form of justice, or that it is perceived as a confirmation of their innocence. What we can say, though, is that state compensation offers recipients a general sense of 'external symbolic value'.

When it comes to the experience of internal and external symbolic value, no differences were found between men and women, victims of different crimes, age groups, and income groups. Nor is there any correlation between symbolic value and the amount of money recipients receive.

What does affect the experience of symbolic value, though, is knowledge about the state's involvement. Those who know the Fund is publicly financed, attribute significantly more internal and external symbolic value to the money they receive, than do those who did not know the state was involved. This result confirms the proposition that involvement of the state is of importance to victims.

Yet, further research is needed to ascertain if state compensation is truly different then reparation through courts, for example. Moreover, due to the explorative character of the present study, further research seems appropriate to unravel the symbolic value of compensation more constructively. First of all, the statements used in the survey to measure symbolic value were open for interpretation: it could have been that respondents were not completely sure what was meant with 'feeling acknowledged' as a victim, for example. Secondly, answers to the statements might have been affected by respondents' social desirability bias.

Nonetheless, the present study provides valuable new insights in the way compensation is perceived by victims of crime. Moreover, by showing how victims attribute symbolic value to the money they perceive, it confirms the hypothesis of renowned sociologist Zelizer that money has social meaning (Zelizer, 1994).

References

Calfee, J.E. & Rubin, P.H. (1992). Some implications of damage payments for nonpecuniary losses. *Journal of External Studies*, *21*, p. 371-412.

Cobley, C. (1998). Financial compensation for victims of child abuse. *Journal of Social Welfare and Family Law, 20(3)*, p. 221-235.

Cohen, M.A. (1988). Pain, suffering, and jury awards: a study of the cost of crime to victims. *Law and Society Review*, 22, pp. 537-555.

Dignan, J. (2005). *Understanding Victims and restorative justice*. Maidenhead, United Kingdom: Open University Press.

Feldthusen, B., Hankivsky, O. & Greaves, L. (2000). Therapeutic consequences of civil actions for damages and compensation claims by victims of sexual abuse. *Canadian Journal of Women and the Law*, 12, pp. 66-116.

Frey, B.S., Benz, M. & Stutzer. A. (2004). Introducing procedural utility: not only what, but also how matters. *Journal of Institutional and Theoretical Economics*, 160(3), p. 377-401._

Freckelton, I. (2004), *Compensation for victims of crime*. In, Kaptein. H & Malsch. M (eds), Crime, Victims, and Justice. Essays on Principles and Practice. Hampshire, England and Burlington, VT: Ashgate Publishing. pp. 31-62.

Janoff-Bulman, R. (1979). Characterological versus behavioral self-blame: Inquiries into depression and rape. *Journal of Personality and Social Psychology*, 37, pp. 1798 –1809.

Kline, P. (1994). *An easy guide to factor analysis*. New York: Routledge.

Lerner, M.J. (2003). The justice motive: where social psychologists found it, how they lost it, and why they may not find it again. *Personality and Social Psychology Review*, 7 (4), pp. 388–399.

Linting, M., Meulman, J.J., Groenen, P.J.F. & Van Der Kooij., A.J. (2007). Nonlinear principal components analysis: Introduction and application. *Psychological Methods*, 12(3), pp. 336–358.

Maercker, A. & Mullder, J. (2004). Social acknowledgement as a victim or survivor: a scale to measure a recovery factor of PTSD. *Journal of Traumatic Stress*, 17 (4), pp. 345–351.

Miers, D. (2007) Looking beyond Great Britain: the development of criminal injuries compensation. In Walklate, S. (Ed.). *Handbook of Victims and Victimology*. Cullompton, UK; Willian Publishing.

Mulder, J.D.W.E. (2009a). How do we compensate a victim's losses? An Economic Perspective. *International Review of Victimology*, vol. 16, pp. 67–87.

Mulder, J.D.W.E. (2009b). *Compensatie na geweld. Wie krijgen er een vergoeding van het Schadefonds Geweldsmisdrijven en wat zijn de effecten van zo'n financiële vergoeding?* Tilburg: Intervict/PrismaPrint.

Mulder, J.D.W.E. (2010), Hoe schadevergoeding kan leiden tot gevoelens van erkenning en gerechtigheid. Lessen uit de praktijk van het Schadefonds Geweldsmisdrijven. *Nederlands Juristenblad*, jrg. 85, pp. 293-296.

O'Connell, M. (2003). *Criminal Injuries Compensation. Revisiting the rationale for state funded compensation for crime victims.* Paper presented at the Innovation: Promising Practices for Victims and Witnesses in the Criminal Justice System – A National Conference, Canberra, 23 – 24 June, 2003.

Okimoto, T. G., & Tyler, T.R. (2007), Is compensation enough? Relational concerns in responding to unintended inequity. *Group Processes & Intergroup Relations*, 10(3), pp. 399-420.

Orth, U. (2003), Punishment goals of crime victims. *Law and Human behavior*, 27(2), pp. 173-186.

Pemberton, A. (2010), Needs of victims of terrorism. In Letschert, R.M., Staiger, I., & Pemberton, A. (eds.). *Assisting victims of terrorism: Towards a European standard of justice*. Dordrecht: Springer.

Relis, T. (2007). "It's not about the money!": a theory on misconceptions of plaintiffs' litigation aims. *Pittsburgh Law Review*, 68(2), p. 1-48.

Veblen, Thorstein. (1899) *Theory of the Leisure Class: An Economic Study in the Evolution of Institutions*. New York: Macmillan.

Viscusi, W.K. (1996). Pain and Suffering: Damages in Search of a Sounder Rationale, *Michigan Law & Policy Review, 1*, p. 141-67.

Wexler, D.B. & Wininck, eds., (1996). *Law in a therapeutic key; developments in the therapeutic jurisprudence*. Durham, North Carolina: Carolina Academic Press.

Young, M. (2003), *Meeting Victim Needs: What is the Role of Victim Compensation in Recovery?* Discussion Paper National Roundtable on Victim Compensation, National Center for Victims of Crime.

Zelizer, V.A. (1994). *The social meaning of money*. New York: BasicBooks.

Appendix 1

Table A1: Reasons for respondents to apply for state compensation, categorized by respondents characteristics

		Financial motive	It was recommended by others	Symbolic reason(s)
Total (N=184)		52%	11%	33%
Gender (N=184)	Female	51%	10%	34%
	Male	54%	12%	32%
Age (N=184)	0-15	46%	8%	46%
	15-25	54%	10%	31%
	25-35	45%	10%	45%
	35-45	57%	14%	28%
	45-55	57%	4%	39%
	55-65	46%	18%	27%
	Older than 65	54%	15%	23%
Annual disposable income (N=161)	Less than 10.000 euro	63%	5%	29%
	10 - 20.000 euro	51%	15%	26%
	20 - 30.000 euro	50%	4%	46%
	30 - 40.000 euro	18%	18%	55%
	More than 40.000 euro	67%	17%	17%
Type of crime	Homicide and manslaughter	100%		
(N=184)	Attempted homicide and manslaughter	81%	6%	19%
	Severe sexual crimes	37%	15%	37%
	Sexual crimes	44%	11%	44%
	Violent theft	49%	4%	40%
	Assault and battery	64%	10%	26%
	Severe assault	50%	23%	23%
	Threat	29%	14%	50%
Type of crime	Less severe	51%	9%	37%
(N=184)	Severe	54%	15%	26%
Total		67%	33%	33%

As Table A1 shows, there are slightly more men applying out of acknowledgement and the like, than there are women. This dissimilarity, however, is not statistically significant (c^2=.134 (1), ns), nor are there any significant differences between groups of age (c^2=4.275 (6), ns).

Victims with incomes above 40.000 euro a year, seem to apply relatively less than average out of symbolic reasons, while those with an income between 30 and 40.000 euro apply relatively often out of such reasons (see A1). Noteworthy seems too, that many victims of severe crimes like attempted homicide and severe assault do not mention symbolic reasons for their application. However, there is no significant difference between severe crimes (homicide and manslaughter, attempted homicide and manslaughter, severe sexual crimes and severe assault) and less severe crimes (sexual crimes, violent theft, assault and battery and threat), like there isn't either between income groups and types of crime (c^2_crime_severe=2.173 (1), ns; Fisher exact test_income=6.368, ns; c^2_type of crime=9.022 (7), ns).

Appendix 2

Table A2: Characteristics of respondents who did and did not know about fund's public function

Crime & respondents' characteristics		Knowledge about fund's public function	No knowledge about fund's public function	Total
Total		64%	36%	100%
Gender (N=217)	Female	64%	36%	100%
	Male	63%	37%	100%
Age (N=217)	0-15	53%	47%	100%
	15-25	78%	22%	100%
	25-35	56%	44%	100%
	35-45	59%	41%	100%
	45-55	53%	47%	100%
	55-65	77%	23%	100%
	Older than 65	41%	59%	100%
Annual disposable income	Less than 10.000 euro	60%	40%	100%
(N=185)	10 - 20.000 euro	60%	40%	100%
	20 - 30.000 euro	74%	26%	100%
	30 - 40.000 euro	67%	33%	100%
	More than 40.000 euro	67%	33%	100%
Type of crime	Homicide and manslaughter	33%	67%	100%
(N=217)	Attempted homicide and manslaughter	75%	25%	100%
	Severe sexual crimes	53%	47%	100%
	Sexual crimes	80%	20%	100%
	Violent theft	60%	40%	100%
	Assault and battery	67%	33%	100%
	Severe assault	63%	38%	100%
	Threat	63%	38%	100%
Type of crime severe/less severe	Less severe	66%	34%	100%
(N=217)	Severe	60%	40%	100%
Reason to file claim	Financial motive	66%	34%	100%
(=184)	It was recommended by others	70%	30%	100%
	Symbolic reason(s)	65%	35%	100%
Total		65%	35%	100%

As Table A2 shows, no significant differences can be found between men and woman (c^2= .048 (1), ns), and different income groups (Fisher exact test_income=2.072, ns) when it comes to knowledge about the Dutch Crime Compensation Fund's public function. It seems that relatively few people aged above 65 knew about the state's involvement, just like victims of homicide and severe sexual crimes (see table 4), yet no apparent differences could be found between groups of age and different crimes (c^2_age= 12.370 (6), ns; c^2_type of crime=9.022 (7), ns; c^2_crime_severe=2.173 (1), ns). Nor was it possible to find a significant difference between the motives respondents had for applying with the Fund (c^2=1.755 (3), ns).

A new economic perspective on victims of crime: homo reciprocans

By J.D.W.E. Mulder

This chapter is a revised version of Mulder, J.D.W.E. (2010), Schadevergoeding: simpelweg een kwestie van verzekeren? TPEdigitaal, 4(4), pp. 61-75.

Introduction

In the night of October 29 2008, a young woman walked home along Amsterdam's scenic canals. She passes a man who asks her for a light. She holds back and tells him she does not smoke. Then suddenly the man grabs her bag and pushes her against a wall. He starts mumbling about sex and does several attempts to rape her, in which he ultimately succeeds. Afterwards, he takes her to the city's main square, where he forces her to withdraw 1000 euro from her banc account. When a group of tourists passes them by the young female manages to escape by clinging on to one of them (Trouw, 1 November 2008).[87]

Needless to say, the young woman was dreadfully cut up by this terrible incident. The rape and robbery impaired her well-being severely. According to Dutch law, she is entitled to sue the offender for compensatory damages.[88] Assuming she is willing to go to court, the question arises what amount of compensation would be reasonable to grant a victim of such a brutal attack.

To date, several economists have dealt with the issue of victim compensation.[89] Although slightly different approaches have been taken, one's conclusions are alike. Economic losses -those that have substitutes or that can be repaired- should be compensated fully, while non-economic losses -pain and suffering- should not be compensated at all (see Cook & Graham, 1977; Friedman, 1982, Arlen 2000; Shavell, 2003; Kaplow & Shavell, 2002; Viscusi

[87] More information about the incident can be found in the (Dutch) verdict of the Amsterdam Court of May 13th, 2009; LJN: BI3717, 13/527312-08 (PROMIS).

[88] See article 6:95 and 6:106 of the Dutch Civil Code, which hold that financial and 'other' harm (6:95) are compensable losses when inflicted intentionally, or in case of physical injury (6:106). Similar arrangements for victims of personal injury exist around the globe. For example in Austria, Belgium, England, France, Germany, Greece, Italy, Poland and Spain (see Rogers, 2000, p. 245-296).

[89] Relatively few economists have dealt with this question, as most legally oriented economists focus on the question how future crimes and accidents can be deterred. Hence, actual victims are seldom part of economic analysis.

1996). Consequently, the young woman robbed and raped in Amsterdam should be fully compensated for her economic losses (the 1000 euro stolen from her banc account), but not in any way for the pain, fear and despair she endured.[90]

Within the legal literature, outcomes like these have been debated heavily (see Croley & Hanson, 1995; Avraham, 2003; Feldman, 1996). The economic analysis of compensation issues has remained the same, nevertheless (see Viscusi, 2000, p. 116; Visscher, 2009, p. 11; VandenBerghe, 2010, p. 61).

In the first section of this paper I will explain how the economic analysis of victim compensation is based on the presumption that human beings, and thus victims, behave as if they are 'homo economicus'. This concept of humans as rational and narrowly self-interested actors has been the leading economic view on human behavior for many decades. As I will argue in paragraph 2, victims of crime have little in common with 'homo economicus'. Extensive psychological research shows that victims are not in the least concerned with their own material self-interest. Instead, they care about how the offending act has affected their social standing and they want retaliate in order to reestablish the social balance.

Interestingly enough, contemporary economic research shows that humans in general have the tendency to retaliate when treated unfairly. As I will explain in paragraph 3, a broad range of behavioral and experimental work shows that people care about how a certain outcome comes about; they tend to reward positive acts of others and to punish negative ones, even when it is at a cost. Based on the significant amount of studies that show prove of this reciprocal type of behavior some economists even speak of 'homo reciprocans' instead of 'homo economicus' (see Fehr & Gachter, 1998; Dohmen, Falk, Huffman & Sunde, 2009).

With this paper I hope to show that victims of crime behave like 'homo reciprocans' does. Moreover, I hope to convince economically oriented scholars dealing with victims issues to leave the traditional economic view behind and to follow in the footsteps of contemporary economic scholars.

Such a change of paradigm will initially lead to many more questions. After all, the clear cut answers provided by the insurance analogy would no longer be valid. Fortunately, experimental research, like that of Fischbacher & Utikal

---

[90] The student actually did receive compensation for her economic *and* non-economic losses. During the criminal trial she asked for a compensation measure through an adhesion process. Hence, on May 13 2009, the criminal court in Amsterdam did not only sentence the offender to 4 years imprisonment, but also ordered him to pay the victim 2000 euro for her pain and suffering and 316 euro for her material damages (see LJN: BI3717, Court Amsterdam, 13/527312-08 (PROMIS)).

(2010) on apologies, seems to allow for rigorous assessment of what truly matters to victims. I, therefore, hope that many scholars will follow their example. If one does, economics will not only be able to protect victims by making sure there are less of them (Faure, 1999, p. D20), but also to provide tools to help those who still bear the burden of victimization.

The paper is structured as follows; paragraph 1 describes the traditional economic view on victim compensation. Paragraph 2 shows the results of numerous psychological studies on victims of crime and how these findings dispute the presumptions underlying the traditional economic perspective. Paragraph 3 explains the work of contemporary economists on fairness and reciprocity. In paragraph 4 I conclude, based on the studies described in sections 2 and 3 that for the study of victim issues economists should change their traditional 'homo economicus' perspective to that of 'homo reciprocans'.

1. *A victim of crime as homo economicus*

If a person incurs losses due to the unlawful acts of another, that person is entitled to go to court and claim financial reparation from the harm-doer. Such compensatory damages are intended to "return the plaintiff as closely as possible to his or her condition before the wrongful act" and "make the plaintiff whole" (Verburg, 2009; Lindenbergh, 2008; King, 2004, p. 165).

But how much compensation do courts need to award in order to make victims actually whole again? Several legal economists have dealt with this question. Following Calabresi (1970) they accept the paradigm whereby the court system and first-party insurance markets act like alternative solutions to the problem of allocating victims' losses (see Frech, 1994; Cooter, 1991; Viscusi, 2000a). One, therefore, argues that the optimal level of compensation equals the efficient level of actuarially fair insurance -which is the coverage an independent, rational and fully informed consumer would have bought in world without tort law- (see Avraham, 2003, p. 6; Viscusi, 2000a, p. 121; Shavell, 2003, ch. 5, p. 10).[91]

Hence, the question 'how to make a victim whole again' is transformed into: 'how much actuarially fair insurance would the victim have bought upfront in a world without tort law'? Consequently, the problem of awarding compensation is changed from an ex post situation regarding *actual* victims, to an ex ante one involving *potential* victims. Or as Friedman (1982, p. 83) puts it: "it all comes down to the ex ante situation in which the potential victims are subject to some probability of injury or death, but the damage has not yet occurred".

---

[91] Not all economic scholars purport the insurance theory, yet they do all take the ex ante view when it comes to assessing victims compensation and reach similar conclusion. See for example Friedman (1982 and 2000).

Subsequently, potential victims are analyzed from a self-interest framework familiar to neo-classical economic models were people are assumed to be exclusively motivated by their material self-interest. Put differently, potential victims are seen as typical rational consumers who spend their money in such a way that their *expected utility* is maximized -they make optimal choices-.

Within the self-interest framework, potential victims are assumed to know they face two states of the world: one in which they will incur losses and one in which they won't. In the state where one does suffer losses, the person's well-being, and with that, its level of utility, is less than what one would experience in the state of the world without losses. Hence, potential victims face a risk of losing well-being in the future.

Since most people are risk-averse, potential victims will want to avoid the risk of losing well-being. Buying insurance is an effective method to do so. After all, buying insurance enables a potential victim to shift wealth from one state of the world to another, ex ante. Moreover, if the potential victim keeps buying insurance until the value of an extra dollar is equal in both states, he becomes indifferent between the two of them. Hence, he is just as well off in the state with losses, as he is in the state without losses (Frech, 1994; Calfee & Rubin, 1992), and maximizes his utility (see Mulder, 2009 for more details about the theory of insurance).

Now in order to find the appropriate levels of court compensation, one has to determine how much insurance potential victims would want to buy in a world without tort law. An important distinction thereby to make is that between economic and non-economic losses. Because, as we will see, economic losses -like lost income and medical expenses- affect a victim's situation differently than non-economic losses do -pain and suffering-.

In case of economic losses a victim will want to restore what is lost and therefore needs money. A victim of bike theft, for example, will need extra dollars to buy a new bike. As result, the victim's marginal utility of wealth increases; the value of an extra dollar rises. So from the potential victim's perspective, it is beneficial to shift dollars from the ex ante situation to the one ex post. Buying insurance allows him to do so. Moreover, if we assume insurance to be actuarially fair, as one generally does,[92] it can be shown that a potential victim benefits the most if he buys *full* insurance (see Cook &

[92] In actuarially fair markets, premiums are equal to expected benefit payments. This could only occur if insurance was costless to administer, losses were statistically independent, there was no moral hazard or adverse selection, and if insurance markets were perfectly competitive. The reason for assuming actuarially fair markets is explained by Frech (1994, p. 263): the assumption of insurance on an actually fair basis is made to rule out moral hazard and adverse selection; by doing so, the focus lies on risk spreading and consequently, the condition for efficient insurance is that the marginal utility of wealth with and without an accident are equal.

Graham, 1977; Mulder, 2009).

As the theory of insurance states that court compensation should equal the amount of insurance that a potential victim would have bought himself in a world without tort law, it follows from the analysis above, that victims should be awarded *full* compensation for their economic losses in court.

In contrast to economic losses, pain and suffering cannot be restored by means of money. There is for instance no amount that will undo the hurt endured by the young woman who was raped along the canals of Amsterdam. Due to the inability to repair or replace non-economic losses, the value of an extra dollar will not increase when one incurs such losses. As a result, scholars reason that victim's marginal utility of wealth stays the same or even decreases (see Friedman, 1982; Viscusi & Evans, 1990).[93] Buying insurance against pain and suffering is thus not something a rational consumer would do (see Cook & Graham, 1977). Consequently, one poses that non-economic losses should not be compensation in court either (see Arlen, 2000; Calfee & Rubin, 1992; Shavell, 2003; Kaplow & Shavell, 2002; Viscusi, 2008; 2000; 1996; Visscher, 2008; VandenBerghe, 2010). Or to cite Cook & Graham: "the goal of full compensation to victims of violent crime or accidents that result in injury or death is not compatible with economic efficiency" (1977, p. 151).

All and all, the economic analogy of buying insurance, provides clear-cut answers to the problem of compensating victims' losses: economic losses should be compensated fully, while non-economic losses shouldn't be compensated at all.

2. *A psycholocigal perspective on victims of crime*[94]

The insurance analogy described in the previous paragraph is used by economists to provide an answer to the question of how much compensation would make victims 'whole again'. This question holds the idea that money is an appropriate tool to repair what victims have lost. But is money truly what victims seek when harm is inflicted on them?

In contrast to individualistic perspective of 'homo economicus', humans are seen as inherently social beings within the psychological literature. This results from the fact that when people are asked what pleasures contribute

---

93 As Viscusi (2000b) explains, the assumption that non-economic losses diminish the marginal utility of wealth lies at the heart of law and economics debate over setting the appropriate level of pain and suffering compensation. A detailed description of this debate can be found in Mulder, 2009.

94 This paragraph depends to a considerable extend on the review on disrespect and the experience of injustice written by Miller and published in 2001 in the Annual Review of Psychology and the references therein.

most to their happiness, the overwhelming majority rate love, intimacy, and social affiliation above wealth or fame, even above physical health. Studies suggest that, of all factors that influence happiness, relatedness is at or very near the top of the list (Argyle 1987; Myers 1999 both cited by Ryan en Deci, 2001, p. 154). Moreover, some theorists have even defined relatedness as a basic human need that is essential for well-being (see Eisenberger & Lieberman, 2005).

Due to the importance of relatedness, humans perceive it particularly painful when another person inflicts harm on them. It's regarded as disrespectful and arouses anger. Or as Miller (1993) puts it: "insults and injuries are understood as gifts, of negative moral value to be sure, but as gifts nonetheless and as such demand *repayment*" (p. 16, as cited by Miller, 2001).

The level of anger that an insult or injury arouses, greatly depends on the degree of disrespect implicit in the offending act. As Greenwell & Dengerink (1973) state, "while attack is an important instigator of aggressive behavior, it appears that the physical discomfort experienced by a person may be subordinate to the symbolic elements that are incorporated into that attack" (p. 70, as cited by Miller, 2001).[95]

The perpetrator's responsibility and his reaction to the victims' harm influence the perceived disrespect to a great extent. The less responsibility the instigator of a harmful action bears for that action, the less disrespectful it will seem and the less anger provokes. A key component of responsibility is intentionality (Heider, 1958 as cited by Miller, 2001). According to Miller (2001) there might even be no more well-established finding in the aggression literature than the finding that unintentional acts of harm provoke less anger and less retaliation than do intentional acts of harm (see Miller, 2001).

Besides intentionality, the perpetrator's reaction to his or her act and its consequences affects the victim's response as well. For one thing, the perpetrator's reaction can provide information about his or her state of mind. In general, harm-doers who communicate to their victims that their actions were inadvertent or uncontrollable, or that they occurred under mitigating circumstances, typically provoke less anger (see Miller, 2001 and the references therein). However, the perpetrator's reaction does more than neutralize the offense by characterizing it as non-intentional, unforeseeable, or unavoidable. It can also convey respect for the victim and affirm his or

[95] A recent study even shows that our experience of pain depends on whether we think someone caused the pain intentionally. Gray & Wegner (2008) show that participants who believed they were getting an electrical shock from another person on purpose, rather than accidentally, rated the very same shock as more painful. Participants seemed to get used to shocks that were delivered unintentionally, but those given on purpose had a fresh sting every time.

her status. The very fact that the perpetrator thinks that the victim is due an explanation signals respect for the victim and tends to diminish the victim's anger (see Miller, 2001 and the references therein).

So an offending act is perceived as disrespectful and triggers an aggressive reaction. But why is it that victims become so angry and want to retaliate? Well, much of the sting of being insulted or exploited derives from the identity implications of the act. According to Miller (2001) people resent to be taken advantage of because it implies to oneself, and to others, that one is the sort of person who can be taken advantage of. Retaliation against the offender, by challenging the threats to identity posed by his or her action, serves to restore the victim's self-image. In fact, the failure to respond to a perceived injustice can actually further diminish the victim, both in the victim's eyes and the eyes of others (Miller, 2001).

A second goal that victims have when they respond to harm-doers, is an educational one. For example, Heider (1958) regarded one of the primary goals of revenge to change the perpetrator's " ...ideas about the relative power, importance, and value of the two persons, as well as his ethical evaluation of these relations" (pp. 267–68). De Waal (1996) reports that even in the animal world there is a tendency "to teach a lesson to those who act negatively" (p. 159). In many cases the lesson that retaliators seek to teach concerns the relative status or moral worth of the offender. By retaliating, victims seek to communicate that it is the offender who deserves contempt, not them (Miller, 2001).

All and all, psychological research shows that victims' response to crime is greatly driven by social factors. An offending act is an affront of one's social standing and one feels the need to reestablish the social balance by means of retaliation. These psychological findings are notably in line with those of contemporary economic studies on fairness, as I will explain in the upcoming paragraph.

3. *homo reciprocans*

From the 1970s onwards, economist have conducted numerous behavioral and experimental studies to test the assumption that humans behave as if they are 'homo economicus'. Simple games have been used to study men's selfishness, for example. A renowned example is that of Forsythe et al. (1994) who randomly paired participants and gave one of two the power to decide on how to allocate a $5 pie among them. The results show that instead of acting like a rational self-interested player who keeps everything to themselves, a majority of the 'dictators' choose to grant the other player between $1 and $2,5 (p. 358).[96]

---

[96] Important to note, is that games like these are played in controlled environments and that

Other examples of studies that have shown that people are not only concerned with their own material wellbeing are those on altruism and solidarity. Selten & Ockenfels (1998), for example, show how people are willing to help others who by chance came to a much worse position than they themselves. A rational self-interested player would not be willing to do so, as he has nothing to gain by helping others. Yet, almost 80% of the subjects in Selten & Ockenfels experiment did show solidarity by offering others a (significant) share of their own pay offs (1998).

As numerous studies showed that humans do not always behave in a selfish manner, the question was raised how men's non-selfish acts could be explained. An important milestone in the process of answering this question was Rabin's 1993 paper on fairness. In this paper he poses that human behavior is often a reaction to the (expected) intentions of others. If we feel that another person has been kind to us, we often have a desire to be kind as well. If we feel that somebody wanted to hurt us, we often have the desire to retaliate even if this is personally costly.

Rabin's paper provoked many scholars to study the effects of fairness. A tool used by many of them is the ultimatum game. In this game two persons have to agree on the division of a fixed sum of money. Person A, the proposer, can make exactly one proposal of how to divide the money. Then person B, the responder, can accept or reject the proposed division. In the case of rejection, both receive nothing, whereas in the case of acceptance, the proposal is implemented.

If both players are rational utility maximizing individuals, one would expect person A to offer B the smallest non-zero amount possible, and that B accepts this. After all, for B it best to accept any demand that gives him any amount whatsoever, and as A knows this, he will offer no more than that. On the other hand, when fairness is of any concern to both players, proposing the smallest non-zero amount seems far from optimal for person A, as this is probably not considered as fair by person B.

So what do ultimatum games tell us? Well, up till now, hundreds of ultimatum games have been played around the world. And a robust result across all these games is that proposals that give the responder less than 30 percent of the available sum are rejected with a very high probability, even when facing high monetary stakes (see Fehr & Gachter, 2000 and the references therein). Most proposers, on the other hand, seem to understand that low offers will be rejected; the equal split is often the modal offer in the ultimatum game (Fehr & Fischbacher, 2003).

---

players, have no knowledge of the person they are paired with, nor is it possible for them to communicate in any way. As a result, the dictator is 'free' to pursue his own interest, if he would want to do so.

The motive generally indicated for the rejection of positive, yet 'low', offers is that responders view them as *unfair* (Fehr & Fischbacher, 2003, p. 786). For a long time, though, it was unclear whether it was just the *outcome* that was thought to be unfair, or whether responders react to unfair *intentions*. Falk, Fehr & Fischbacher (2008) provide evidence of the latter. Their experiment shows that people do not only take the distributive consequences of an action into account but also the *intention* it signals when judging the fairness of an action.

Bohnet & Zeckhauser (2004) arrived at similar conclusions. Their experimental results indicate that bad outcomes which are intentionally chosen, are evaluated lower by subjects than equivalent outcomes that result by chance. According to the authors, it matters to participants how a certain outcome comes about; if another person knowingly hurts them, they feel betrayed and incur 'betrayal costs'. If the outcome is due to chance though, no one is to blame, and no additional costs are suffered.

Due to the large body of evidence on reciprocal behavior scholars have suggested to replace 'homo economicus' for 'homo reciprocans' (see for example Fehr & Gachter, 1998; Dohmen, Falk, Huffman & Sunde, 2009). Seeing how the behavior of victims of crime is in line with that of 'homo reciprocans' I believe such a change would at least be appropriate in the case of victims' issues. I will explain myself in more detail in the upcoming paragraph.

4. *Conclusion: Victims of crime as homo reciprocans*

That humans have the tendency to retaliate when treated unfairly has been proven by hundreds of studies performed around the world. During none of these studies, at least to my knowledge, participants have ever left the laboratory with less than they came with. Nevertheless, 40% and sometimes even more than 50% of the participants exhibit a reciprocal effort pattern (Fehr & Fishbacher, 2002, p. C6).

What if participants lost some of their belongings to one of the other players during an experiment? Would the tendency to retaliate become even more apparent? Knowing that humans are significantly more averse to losses than they are attracted to same-size gains (Rabin, 1998), it probably would. After all, if people tend to retaliate when they do not get a fair share, image what they will do if someone else takes what is actually theirs!

People victimized by crime incur considerable losses. Not during an experiment, but in real life. As could be expected, extensive research has shown that victims become angry as a result of that loss and want to teach the offender a lesson. Put differently; the majority of victims exhibit a reciprocal effort pattern.

So why would one keep presuming victims of crime to behave like 'homo economicus'? There is no prove, at least to my knowledge, that victims only care about their own material well-being. The prove they care about others and their own social standing, however, is abundant. Therefore, I want to propose a change of paradigm: when it comes to victims' issues economists and economically oriented scholars should use the concept of 'homo reciprocans' instead of 'homo economicus'.

Changing prospective has consequences, of course. The clear cut answers provided by the insurance analogy as described in paragraph 1, for example, would no longer be valid. Instead, much more research is needed. Let me explain. The introduction of this paper describes how a young female was raped on one of Amsterdam's canals. According to Dutch law she is entitled to financial compensation. Such compensatory damages are intended to "return the plaintiff as closely as possible to his or her condition before the wrongful act" and "make the plaintiff whole" (Verburg, 2009; Lindenbergh, 2008; King, 2004, p. 165).

Up till now, one tried to determine appropriate levels of compensation by monetizing the victim's loss of wellbeing, which is the difference between a victim's wellbeing in the ex-ante en ex post situation (see the insurance theory explained in paragraph 1, and studies like those of Cohen, 1988; Miller, Cohen & Rossman, 1993; Miller, Cohen, & Wiersema, 1996; Cohen, Rust, Steen & Tidd, 2004; Dolan, Loomes, Peasgood, & Tsuchiya, 2005; Atkinson, Healey & Mourato, 2005). Although this approach might lead to an appropriate financial approximation of a victim's losses, it does not consider the most important element of incurring a loss, namely whether it was caused intentionally or not. Nor does it provide any opportunity for victims to respond to the offender. Hence, it seems very unlikely that victims will be made whole again by just receiving the financial equivalent of their losses.

Taking the perspective of 'homo reciprocans' would prevent us from focusing solely on the victim's private, ex ante and ex post, situation. Instead, we would be forced to take a broader view. After all, if we assume that victims respond to the behavior of others, we need to study how a victim's losses were caused and how one feels the need to respond to that. Consequently, compensation would no longer be a goal in itself. Compensatory damages could, however, be an effective *means* to make victims whole again. After all, as shown in chapter 3 and 4 of this thesis, financial compensation does affect a recipient's wellbeing in a positive way.

How and when compensation helps victims to become whole again is something that should be studied in more detail. It is unknown, for instance, under which circumstances compensation is an appropriate means and when not. Experimental designs, like the dictator and ultimatum games described earlier, might be a helpful tool to do so. Recent work on the effects of apologies provides an interesting example. Fischbacher & Utikal (2010) show by means of an ultimatum game that victims expect an apology and punish if they do not receive one. This result is in line with the general assumption that victims appreciate or even need an apology (see for example Strang & Sherman, 2003). Yet, what Fischbacher & Utikal also show is that an apology does not help after clearly intentionally committed offenses. On the contrary, after such offenses harm doers do better not to apologize since sending an apology in this situation strongly increases punishment compared to remaining silent (Fishbacher & Utikal, 2010).

Fischbacher & Utika's experimental design provides an interesting example of how experimental studies allow for rigorous assessment of the specific motives underlying reciprocity and punishment (Frey & Fishbacher, 2003). Yet, it is still one of the very few studies in this direction. I, therefore, hope that many others economically oriented scholars will follow their excellent example. If one does, economics will not only be able to protect victims by making sure there are less of them (Faure, 1999, p. D20), but also to provide tools to help those who still bear the burden of victimization.

References

Arlen, J., (2000), Tort Damages, in B. Bouckaert en G. De Geest, eds., *Encyclopaedia of Law and Economics*, Vol. II, pp. 682-734, Edward Elgar; Cheltenham.

Atkinson, G., Healey, A. & Mourato, S. (2005). Valuing the costs of violent crime: a stated preference approach. *Oxford Economic Papers*, 57 (4), pp. 559-585.

Avraham, R., 2005, Should Pain-and-Suffering Damages be Abolished from Tort Law? More Experimental Evidence, University of Toronto Law Journal, 55, pp. 941–979.

Bohnet, I., & Zeckhauser, R. (2004), Trust, Risk and Betrayal, *Journal of Economic Behavior*
and Organization, 55, pp. 467-485.

Calabresi, G. (1970), The Cost of Accidents: A Legal and Economic Analysis. New Haven, CT: Yale University Press.

Calfee, J.E. en P.H. Rubin, (1992), Some Implications of Damage Payments for Nonpecuniary Losses, *Journal of Legal Studies*, 21, pp. 371–412.

Cohen, M.A. (1988). Pain, suffering, and jury awards: a study of the cost of crime to victims. *Law and Society Review*, 22, pp. 537-555.

Cohen, M. A., Rust, R.T., Steen, S., Tidd, S.T. (2004). Willingness-to-Pay for crime control programs; *Criminology* 42(1): pp. 86-106.

Cooter, R.D. (1991), Economic Theories of Legal Liability. *The Journal of Economic Perspectives*, 5(3), pp. 11-30.

Cook, P.J. & Graham, D.A. (1977), The Demand for Insurance and Protection: The Case of Irreplaceable Commodities, *The Quarterly Journal of Economics*, 91 (1), pp. 143–156.

Dohmen,T., Falk, A., Huffman, D. & Sunde, U. (2009), Homo reciprocans: survey evidence on behaviourial outcomes. *The Economic Journal*, 119 (March), pp. 592–612.

Dolan, P., Edlin, R., Tsuchiya, A., Wailoo, A., (2007), It ain't what you do, it's the way that you do it: Characteristics of procedural justice and their importance in social decision-making, *Journal of Economic Behavior and Organization*, 64, pp. 157-70.

Dolan, P., Loomes, G., Peasgood, T. & Tsuchiya, A. (2005), Estimating the intangible victims costs of violent crime. *Brit. J. Crimonology*, 45, p. 958-76.

Eisenberger, N.I. en M. D. Lieberman, (2005), Why It Hurts to Be Left Out. The Neurocognitive Overlap Between Physical and Social Pain. In K. D. Williams, J. P. Forgas, en W. von Hippel, eds., *The Social Outcast: Ostracism, Social Exclusion, Rejection, and Bullying* (pp. 109-127), New York: Cambridge University Press.

Falk A., Fehr, E. & Fischbacher, U. (2008), Testing Theories of Fairness—Intentions matter, *Games and Economic Behavior*, 62 (1), pp. 287-303

Fehr, E. & Schmidt, K.M. (2006), The Economics of Fairness, Reciprocity and Altruism - Experimental Evidence and New Theories, in S. Kolm & Jean Mercier Ythier (ed.), *Handbook on the Economics of Giving, Reciprocity and Altruism*, Elsevier, pp. 615-691.

Fehr, E. & Fischbacher, U. (2002). Why Social Preferences Matter. The impact of non-selfish motives on competition, Cooperation and incentives. *Economic Journal*, 112, pp. C1-33.

Fehr, E. & Fischbacher, U. (2003). The nature of human altruism. *Nature*, 425, pp. 785-91.

Fehr, E. & Gachter, S. (2000), Fairness and Retaliation: The Economics of Reciprocity. *Journal of Economic Perspectives*, 14; pp. 159-181.

Fehr, E. & Gachter, S. (1998), Reciprocity and economics: The economic implications of Homo reciprocans. *European Economic Review*, 42; pp. 845-59.

Fischbacher, U. & Utikal, V. (2010). *On the acceptance of apologies*. Working paper no 53, June 2010. Research Paper Series Thurgau Institute of Economics and Department of Economics at the University of Konstanz.
Forsythe, R., Horowitz, J. L., Savin, N. E. & Sefton, M. (1994), Fairness in simple bargaining experiments. *Game Econ. Behav.* 6,pp. 347–369.

Frech, H.E. (1994), State-dependent utility and the tort system as insurance: strict liability versus negligence. *International Review of Law and Economics*, 14, pp. 261-271.

Friedman, D., (1982), What is 'Fair Compensation' for Death or Injury? *International Review of Law and Economics*, vol 2, pp. 81–93.

Friedman, D., (2000), *Law's order*. Princeton, New Jersey: Princeton University Press.

Gray, K. & Wegner, D.M (2008). The Sting of Intentional Pain. *Psychological Science*, 19 (12).

Heider, F. (1958). *The Psychology of Interpersonal Relations*. New York: Wiley & Sons.

Kaplow, L. & Shavell, S. (2002), Economic Analysis of Law. In A.J. Auerbach and M. Feldstein, eds, *Handbook of Public Economics*, vol. 3, pp. 1661–1784. Elsevier; The Netherlands.

King, J.H. (2004). Pain and Suffering, Noneconomic Damages, and the Goals of Tort Law. 57 *SMU L. Rev.*, pp. 163–210.

Lindenbergh, S.D. (2008), *Smartengeld, tien jaar later*. Deventer: Kluwer.

Miller, D.T., (2001), Disrespect and experience of injustice, *Annual Review of Psychology*, 52, pp. 527-53.

Mulder, J.D.W.E., (2009), How do we compensate a victim's losses? An Economic Perspective. *International Review of Victimology*, vol. 16, pp. 67–87.

Rabin, M. (1993), Incorporating Fairness Into Game Theory and Economics. *The American Economic Review.* 83, pp. 1281-1302.

Rabin, M. (1998), Psychology and Economics. *Journal of Economic Literature,* 36 (1), pp. 11-46.

Rogers, W.V.H. (2000), Damages for non-pecuniary loss in a comparative perspective. Wenen, New York, Springer.

Ryan, R. M. & E.L. Deci, (2001), On happiness and human potentials: a review of research on hedonic and eudaimonic well-being, *Annu. Rev. Psychol,* 52, pp. 141–166.

Selten, R. & Ockenfels, A. (1998), An experimental solidarity game. *Journal of Economic Behavior & Organization,* 34, pp. 517-539.

Shavell, S., (2003), Economic Analysis of Incident Law. NBER Working Paper Nr. 9482; www.nber.org/papers/w9483. Dit paper is gelijk aan de hoofdstukken over 'accident law' in: S. Shavell, Foundations of Economic Analysis of Law. Cambridge, Massachusetts: Harvard University Press.

Trouw, 1 november 2008, Beroving en verkrachting in centrum Amsterdam: http://www.trouw.nl/nieuws/nederland/article1891682.ece/Beroving_en_verkrachting_in_centrum_Amsterdam_.html

Vandenberghe, A.S., (2010), Non-Discrimination in the Common Principles of European Contract Law, In P. Larouche en F. Chirico (eds.), *Economic Analysis Of The Dcfr: The Work Of The Economic Impact Group Within The CoPECL Network Of Excellence.* Sellier European Law Publishers.

Verburg, G.J.M. (2009), *Vaststelling van smartengeld.* Deventer: Kluwer.

Vidmar N. (2000). Retribution and revenge. In J. Sanders & VL Hamilton (eds.) *Handbook of Justice Research in Law.* New York: Kluwer Acad.

Viscusi, W.K., (1996), Pain and Suffering: Damages in Search of a Sounder Rationale, *Michigan Law & Policy Review,* 1, pp. 141–167.

Viscusi, W.K., (2000a), Misuses and Proper Uses of Hedonic Values of Life, *Journal of Forensic Economics,* 13, pp. 111–125.

Viscusi, W.K., (2000b), The Value of Life in Legal Context. *American Law and Economics Review,* vol. 2, nr. 1, pp. 195–222.

Viscusi, W.K. en W.N. Evans, (1990), Utility Functions That Depend on Health Status: Estimates and Economic Implications, *American Economic Review*, 80, pp. 353–374.

Visscher, L.T., (2009), Tort Damages, in M.G. Faure, ed., *Tort Law and Economics, Volume 1 Encyclopedia of Law and Economics*, Second Edition, Cheltenham, UK: Edward Elgar, pp. 153-200.

Waal, de F. (1996). Good Natured: The Origins of Right and Wrong in Humans and Other Animals. Cambridge, MA: Harvard Univ. Press